HOCKEY MOMS

HOCKEY MOMS

The Heart of the Game

THERESA BAILEY AND **TERRY MARCOTTE**
WITH A FOREWORD BY **BOBBY RYAN**

Collins

Published by Collins, an imprint of HarperCollins Publishers Ltd

First edition

HarperCollins Publishers Ltd
Bay Adelaide Centre, East Tower
22 Adelaide Street West, 41st Floor
Toronto, Ontario, Canada
M5H 4E3

www.harpercollins.ca

Library and Archives Canada Cataloguing in Publication
Title: Hockey moms : the heart of the game / Theresa Bailey and Terry Marcotte ; with
a foreword by Bobby Ryan. Names: Bailey, Theresa, author. | Marcotte, Terry, author.
Description: First edition. Identifiers: Canadiana (print) 20220278334 | Canadiana (ebook)
20220278369 | ISBN 9781443465762 (hardcover) | ISBN 9781443465786 (EPUB)
Subjects: LCSH: Hockey for children—Anecdotes. | LCSH: Mother and child—Anecdotes.
| LCSH: Hockey players—Family relationships—Anecdotes. | LCSH: Hockey—Anecdotes. |
LCSH: Parenting—Anecdotes. |
LCGFT: Anecdotes. Classification: LCC GV848.5.A1 B35 2022 | DDC
796.962092/552—dc23

Printed and bound in the United States of America
LSC/H 9 8 7 6 5 4 3 2 1

For Kobe, Kellen, and Shea. I love watching you play.
—TB

For hockey moms everywhere. Thanks for all you do.
—TM

CONTENTS

FOREWORD

BY BOBBY RYAN

Bobby Ryan played thirteen seasons in the NHL. His final game was in 2021 as a member of the Detroit Red Wings.

I WISH MY MOTHER, Melody Stevenson, were here to tell her story. She died of cancer in 2016. Without her, I know without a doubt that I would not have made it to the NHL. I'm really not sure what would have become of my life if it wasn't for my mom.

Her story with my dad was complicated. That's putting it mildly. My dad was hard on both of us, and it got pretty bad when I was very young and my dad assaulted my mom. She was taken away in an ambulance. Dad left in handcuffs. He faced a series of charges, including attempted murder. I was ten years old when he was released on bail and decided to take off and became a fugitive.

Mom always did what she had to do so things would work out with Dad and our family would remain together, so she was on board when

Dad jumped bail. We left our home in Philadelphia to rejoin him and started fresh in California under assumed names. That's when my name changed from Bobby Stevenson to Bobby Ryan.

It goes without saying, life was challenging for all of us. There was a constant fear that our double lives would be discovered. We got away with it for a couple of years. I was twelve when the FBI tracked down Dad, arrested him, and sent him to prison. He was sentenced to five years for aggravated assault and jumping bail. After that, it was just Mom and me.

For three years, Mom worked sixteen-hour days, holding down two full-time jobs. She ran herself ragged just to keep us afloat. I never once said, "Mom, you don't have to do this." I probably should have. Honestly, if she didn't do it, we weren't making rent. The lights weren't staying on. We weren't eating. We were living in southern California, just outside Manhattan Beach. It took everything from her just to pay the bills. You could see how all the miles and the hours were taking a toll on her, mentally and physically. But she kept grinding and tried to give me every opportunity to succeed in life. My biggest admiration for her is for how she stayed the course.

Through it all, I had hockey, and Mom made sure the game never left me. One of her jobs was managing the local hockey rink. Because hockey was everything to me, it was also everything to her. She was able to schedule her shifts around my games, and when I played, she was usually there for me, watching.

Because of all we went through, I think Mom and I had a different kind of relationship. She was still a mother. She still had to rein me in at times to teach me to be a young man. As we found our way through our new lives, we became each other's best friends. We didn't have any other choice. It was just the two of us.

Even after Dad was sent to prison, we continued to hold on to the family secret. And Mom was really the only person I could talk to about the double lives we were living. Really, why bother to share all that we had been through? But hockey is a small world. And eventually, people realized that Bobby Ryan of California and Bobby Stevenson of Philadelphia were the same person. We never talked about it with other people and kept living in our bubble.

Through all this, I learned plenty from Mom. One of the best things she taught me was to be a professional. Show up on time. Do your best. Do what needs to be done. I learned that lesson just by watching her do so much to look after me. We were dealt a pretty bad hand, and I saw how she responded. You may think your children don't notice what you do for them. Trust me, they do.

Mom would always tell me, "Never cheat the work." I've tried to live my life like that. For a good period of my NHL career, I have done that. I got away from it for a while, but I feel like I'm back to it now. I got that from Mom.

As a hockey mom, she never pushed me, although if you were to ask her now, I think she would say she was a little too lenient with me. She knew I was pushed plenty at an early age by my dad. Mom tried to give me the space to figure things out on my own. She was never hard on me. If she was disappointed by the outcome of a game or because of the way I played, she never let on.

Mom always had my back, and I knew that. I had had a horrible billet experience in Detroit during my final year of minor hockey. She wasn't going to let that happen again, and she made sure it didn't. She moved to Owen Sound, Ontario, with me for my first year of junior hockey in the OHL, to make sure I was safe and protected. She said there was no way she was going to let me go it alone unless she was sure I was with a good family. Mom sacrificed so much so I could follow my dreams. That first year in junior, she put her life on hold for me.

My second season in Owen Sound, I moved in with a terrific family. It was my draft year. I saw a real opportunity to make it in hockey, and I wasn't going to waste it. I put my head down and worked harder than ever. Always in the back of my mind, I was thinking of Mom. I was determined not to let her down. I remember the great feeling when I was drafted second overall by Anaheim in the 2005 NHL Entry Draft. It's one of my favourite memories with her. It was a life-changing moment. And we experienced it together.

If Mom were here, I hope she would say it has all been worth it. I know she would be proud of me. I think if she were talking to other moms, she would tell them to stick with it. She would say, "If you put your kids in a position to succeed, they will find a way." She would tell moms to cheer for their kids. And support them. That's what she did for me.

Mom always allowed me to enjoy my good games. After bad games, she would encourage me to work on things that needed improving. She was never hard on me; she was patient and understanding. That would be my advice to moms. Be a little more understanding, even if you're frustrated with how your child is performing. That was my mom's approach with me, and it went a long way.

I know Mom would love this book paying tribute to the dedication and sacrifice of hockey moms, even though she never asked that her story be told. Far too often, fathers get all the credit in hockey. So often, you see stories about dads and what they've done to help their kids at the rink. It is good to see stories of mothers finally being shared, including the story of my mother.

Mom, I wish so much you were here to enjoy it.

INTRODUCTION

BY THERESA BAILEY

The Journey to Hockey Mom

MY INTEREST IN THE hockey world started early. I cried while my brother was practising, and my parents put me on the ice too so I'd shut up. I was two years old at the time.

As I got older, I knew something was off in the sport that everyone got so excited about. There was no girls' hockey at the time, just ringette. Even at three and four, I wondered why girls had to play hockey with half a stick. Playing with half a stick, as I called it, didn't appeal to me. So I ended up in figure skating. Hockey became a game I'd watch from the sidelines but as an adult all but consumed my life.

Hockey moms joke that the rink is our second home. For me, that has always rung true. I competed in figure skating until my second year at the University of Ottawa, so I was on the ice from age two until I was twenty. That's thousands of hours logged on the ice myself, plus thousands more as a spectator at rinks across Ontario. Like many sisters, I initially complained about being dragged to the rink to watch my older brother, but eventually, I began to appreciate that I could watch my friends and hang out with them at the rink. We were there all the time.

It's what my family did. Rinks for skating. Rinks for minor hockey. OHL games. Memorial Cups. As for most hockey families, it became a lifestyle. My family lived sports. Hockey and baseball consumed most of our time, and add in figure skating for me. Most of my childhood memories revolve around teams, sports friends, competitions, ballparks, and hockey tournaments. Team meals and packed coolers. Road trips. You can't be at the rink this much without your parents being fully invested, and mine certainly were.

My father, Harold Bailey, was a strong athlete and played hockey well into his twenties. He later got into coaching, then was on our minor hockey executive in several roles, including president. I remember the late-night phone calls to resolve the same issues back then that I dealt with thirty years later. He was and still is known and respected in our small community as someone who is always giving back. I learned from the best.

And then, there was my mom. A lot has been said about the crazy hockey mom stereotype. It's not something I have ever accepted because, for me, it didn't exist. My mom, Karen, is solid and remains a strong presence in our community. She knows about hockey, about how it is played, and the work it takes to make it happen. She commands respect by being respectful and getting things done. She is always getting things done. For years she was deeply involved with our minor hockey association. She eventually became secretary and then president, just as my father had been before her. My brother, Jason, became president when his children began to play. And I took my turn as president of the Centre Hastings Minor Hockey Association for four years, then later was a board member for Quinte Regional Minor Hockey Association. We give back; it's in our family DNA.

For us, hockey didn't stop at our local rink. My parents had season tickets to the Belleville Bulls of the Ontario Hockey League for thirty years. Some of my earliest memories involve watching the Bulls play from my mother's lap. Since 1996, they've also been season ticket holders for the Ottawa Senators. They organized and divided up their tickets among friends in our community until COVID-19 changed all that. They have been doing this hockey thing forever.

I had no choice. It was inevitable that the hockey lifestyle would be in my blood. And now, as my mom bangs her cowbells together, cheering for her grandchildren, our family hockey journey continues.

Anywhere there is a patch of outdoor ice or a rink, you will find stories like mine. This is how the hockey culture was born. And it is why it will continue to grow long after we are gone.

I BECAME A HOCKEY mom when Kobe, the oldest of my three children, started playing at the age of three. His first game was in a recreational house league—the Bruce Lee House League, which my parents founded in 1991 and continue to run today. The league is my parents' way of making the game they love inclusive and affordable in our community. Teams play a one-hour game every week, and they get refreshments after every game. And, of course, players get a trophy or token at the end of the year. All for just sixty-five dollars a player. For years, my parents took players on the two-hour bus trip to an Ottawa Senators game and have been responsible for countless first NHL experiences. There is nothing like watching kids and parents experience their first NHL game.

My life as a hockey mom changed dramatically when Kobe moved into competitive hockey. During Kobe's novice year, he was seven and playing with a very skilled group of eight-year-olds. In a game on a Friday afternoon three hours away from home, he received one twenty-second shift in the entire game. It was the first game of a tournament and about four minutes into the first period. One twenty-second shift, and his game was over as the team went for the win.

Kobe didn't really understand what was happening. He would get to the door and be pushed back down to the centre of the bench, behind all the other players, where he would drink from the water bottle once again. Even I didn't know how to handle such an extreme shortening of the bench, especially with children this young. To avoid drama or having to talk to anyone else, I left by a side door and asked Kobe's father to meet him in the lobby. I wonder now, would anyone really know how to handle that?

Meanwhile, the players getting the most ice time on the team were getting yelled at by parents from the opposing team. "Get him!" "Take him out!"

And this is the juxtaposition of hockey. I was hurting for my son because he was hurting—he didn't understand why he didn't get to play. And the moms of the players getting all the ice time couldn't understand why anyone would want to "get" their kids. Sometimes it all seemed almost unmanageable.

There is no guidebook to being a hockey parent. We all struggle with solutions: when to get involved, and when to remain silent so we don't further hurt our children. I remember wondering aloud, "How would the mother of an NHL star handle this?"

That question led me to create the website and social media platforms Canadian Hockey Moms, and that's when the idea of this book began to take root. Even back then, my goal was to talk to hockey moms to ask them how they manage to keep all the moving parts together for their families, and how they deal with the controversy and chaos that come with a very intense world. Then I wanted to share that information with everyone else. How do you deal with controversy when the coaches are your friends? How do you break down barriers in hockey to make sure everyone has a chance to play? How do you make sure teams are inclusive? How do you talk to coaches without jeopardizing your child's future? How do you separate hockey politics from the moral obligation to intervene when something is actually wrong? These are the questions hockey moms ask themselves, the questions that can keep us up at night.

For me, there is something almost spiritual about sport. There is a synchronous energy you can feel when teams are working together on the ice. You can feel it when fans are cheering on their teams. You can feel it when you are huddled around the TV, watching the playoffs or the Olympic gold medal game. You can feel it in the goosebumps and the adrenaline rush and the joy and connectedness with those around you. I have felt it many, many times through my children's involvement in minor hockey.

I've spent years fascinated by the sense of community and the hockey culture I've experienced through Kobe's, Kellen's, and Shea's journeys with seven associations and more than three dozen teams. But all this time, one thing has been missing: I have never seen a book about the experiences and contributions of hockey moms, the women behind it all who make it happen.

You can't help but be inspired by the women you meet along the way. I have seen girls and women fight to find a place in hockey. I have seen female coaches standing tall in a sea of men. I have seen women fight for the inclusion of everyone. I have seen the celebration of first goals and the heartache of first cuts from a team. And I have seen a lot of sacrifice.

I wanted to tell these women's stories. A few interviews in, I asked my friend Terry Marcotte, a respected sports journalist, for his help. And as we reached out to more mothers in search of diverse stories, we heard from moms who have raised the best players in the world and moms who never in a million years believed their children would take a step on the ice—but they did.

Together, Terry and I have written this book as a celebration of the hearts, souls, and contributions of hockey moms. These women have forged a place in a game that has traditionally been very white and very male. By telling the stories of our hockey moms, we begin to fill the holes left in the fabric of hockey culture, where most stories have been told by men about men. Now we can round out those stories with the perspective of the mothers.

I consider this book my love letter to hockey moms.

CHAPTER 1

Raising the Best

"Enjoy the journey, because it goes by fast."
—Kelly McDavid

THE MINOR HOCKEY CAREER of perhaps the greatest player in the game today began with a simple white lie. Connor McDavid was four years old, a year too young to play minor hockey in his hometown of Newmarket, Ontario, about forty-five minutes north of Toronto. Already hockey had become an obsession for Connor, and he so badly wanted to be part of a team. He was on skates when he was two, and he could fly. Down in the family basement, Connor would put on Rollerblades and spend hours trying to score on his grandmother. Connor McDavid was already good, so his mother, Kelly, wondered why not let him play?

Kelly and her husband, Brian, did what had to be done to get Connor on a team. They took an unconventional route and got creative with his birth year on the registration form. Just like that, Connor

McDavid had a head start on the game he would come to dominate. If he were head and shoulders above other kids his own age in school, Kelly reasoned, he would be put into a higher grade. She asked, "Why should hockey be any different?"

Hockey was pretty much a new world for Kelly McDavid. Skiing was her preferred sport. The fact that she'd met Brian through a hockey connection was almost a fluke. She was along for the ride with her sister, who was dating a teammate of Brian's. Kelly and Brian were set up on a date, hit it off, and eventually got married. They had two boys. Cameron was born in 1993, and Connor came along four years later.

It wasn't long before hockey came to define the McDavids. Back when they were all starting out and just trying to find their feet, Kelly had her fingers crossed for a different direction. "At the time, our family was more of a skiing family, so I hoped our kids would end up as skiers. They both started off with skiing and hockey. And, of course, we know the one they picked." They were now a hockey family.

Brian McDavid was more than okay that his boys picked hockey. He is, through and through, a hockey guy. Unlike Kelly, Brian grew up in rinks. He was a good hockey player, but never good enough to have a shot at pro hockey. He became a minor hockey coach, and he did plenty to help Connor fuel his passion. It was Brian who turned the driveway into a hockey training ground. He set up obstacle courses and shooting targets so his two boys could develop their hockey skills. Connor couldn't get enough of it. The family driveway and garage became an important training facility for a young player who would go on to greatness.

Kelly could see the pull hockey had on her boys, and she saw her job as keeping balance in the family. "I think, for me, I was more the mom, the caregiver. I was more worried about their health, their eating, their sleeping, and making sure they had good balance in their lives. For Connor, right from the get-go, he talked, slept, and breathed hockey. For Cameron, it was more of a social thing for him at first. It was just go out and have a good time and hang out with your buddies."

In fact, when Cameron was just seven, he was all set to move on from hockey. He was a kid who wanted to do everything, and when he told his mom he wanted more time to do other things, she understood completely. In the end, he didn't quit. As summer rolled around, Cameron spent hours and hours each day playing ball hockey.

"Are you really sure you want to quit?" she asked him. Cameron would go on to play another decade of competitive hockey, tapping out after Junior A.

Both her boys had talent. While Kelly didn't have a hockey background, she could see early on that Connor's commitment to the sport was on a different level. "It was all about winning for Connor. He just got so much joy when they'd win and be so mad when they lost. He was an intense kid, so if they started to lose, he'd start to cry. He'd be on the ice and start to cry. He just hated losing. That stressed me. We continued to say to Connor, 'Yes, you can be upset about losing. But you can't be upset about it this long. You've got to park it after a while.' And he couldn't."

Kelly McDavid wondered if her son was becoming too hockey obsessed. It helped, of course, that he had endless talent. He was well beyond other kids his age. Other than the private outbursts when he lost, Connor was showing a rare maturity that let Kelly know he would figure things out. "I often say he is an old soul in a young body. He is mature beyond his years. He just gets it, and he got it at a very young age: I'm very good at this. He puts a lot of pressure on himself. But he never tries to make anyone else feel bad if they're not good at it. He never boasted or bragged about it in any way. I just think he loves to play hockey."

"Divide and conquer" is how she describes the strategy that hockey parents know all too well. The McDavids were flying in all directions. For the most part, Brian coached Connor, and they headed off together to games and practices, while Kelly was more often travelling with Cameron. Both parents worked full-time. It was busy. And this was where Kelly excelled. Like many hockey moms, she became the general manager of her hockey family. She drew up schedules, made meals, and watched over homework. She was, she says, "the constant nagging mother."

"Our kids knew, and it was very clear, if they wanted to play hockey, they had to do well at school, and they had to finish their homework." Cameron would often get distracted, and homework would be a last-minute rush. But he would always get it done. Connor would get home and bury himself in schoolwork, and finish quickly, without too much fuss. The less time he spent on homework, he figured, the more time he had for hockey.

The homework. The meals. Everything about hockey, Kelly McDavid learned as she went along. She had not been brought up in a hockey family, nor did she have aspirations to be part of one.

Now she was a full-on hockey mom. There was Connor. And there was Cameron, who was eight years old and playing on his first-ever competitive team.

She remembers the start of that season. The schedules came out. The team was going to be playing weekend tournaments. "There are games on Fridays?" she asked. "I went to the coach and said, 'I'm not sure if you're aware, but the kids don't have a PA day on Friday, and I see here they have to be at the rink.' He looked at me like I had two heads. My first introduction, I must have looked like that crazy mom in the dressing room, going to the coach and complaining they had to take a day off school."

Kelly learned that things quickly get intense for competitive hockey families. She knew it was only a matter of time before Connor would be joining his brother in the competitive world. For now, house league was all that was available to four-year-old Connor McDavid, who was already showing signs that he would be special.

While other kids were still learning how to skate and navigate off-sides and faceoffs, Connor was weaving around them like the puck was glued to his stick. The game was easy. Almost too easy. That's when whispers began spreading around the rink that little Connor was a puck hog. Those whispers reached Kelly's ears, and they bothered her. She and Brian knew another season of this would be a disaster.

When Connor turned six, his parents applied to have him join a competitive team for kids who were one year older. Hockey organizations everywhere face this dilemma with dread. Often the application comes from parents who wrongly believe their kid is special. Anyone who saw a young Connor McDavid could see he was different from all the other kids, but it didn't matter. The answer came back no; rules are rules. The McDavids were told if Connor joined competitive hockey a year early, a seven-year-old would lose his chance to play higher-level hockey.

"We understood. But how do you continue developing them when they are so good?" was Kelly's concern.

The McDavids found a compromise in a neighbouring league. Connor would still play house league, but with nine-year-olds. He was that good.

For Kelly and Brian, it was a tough decision. How do you give Connor the best opportunity to develop his obvious gifts without putting him in a situation that could hurt him in other areas? His hockey skills were certainly there. He was still the best player on the ice. When his team needed a goal, he was called on to score it. It put a lot of pressure on a young boy who was trying to fit in with boys who were three years older. Connor was feeling the pressure.

"It was a tough year," Kelly says matter-of-factly.

Kelly did her best to keep the big picture in sight. What she saw in Connor was a young boy capable of so much, and wanting so much, who needed a reset. He had talent. He had passion. But dominating against older kids who simply didn't have his talent or drive wasn't the best fit.

"What do you want from this?" Kelly asked Connor one day as her son sat on the living room floor, oozing with frustration.

For Connor it was an easy question to answer. Despite his youth, he had already set some lofty goals for himself. He wanted to play in the

OHL as a fifteen-year-old. He wanted to win a Memorial Cup, then become a first overall draft pick in the NHL. He wanted to win a Stanley Cup, then be named to the Hockey Hall of Fame. To meet these targets, Connor knew he had to play against better players. He wanted to play competitive hockey as soon as humanly possible.

Kelly spent a lifetime in HR and understood how to motivate people. She could see that Connor responded well to specific goals. To get Connor out of his funk that season, Kelly and Connor sat down and worked out a path to help him get to where he wanted to be. The two of them used a piece of paper and created a set of stairs with the dates of Connor's games for the rest of the season on each step. At the top of the staircase was the ultimate goal for the year: joining a competitive AAA hockey team. That piece of paper, with the stairs carefully drawn, was taped inside a cupboard door where Connor could keep track of his progress. He'd come home from games and cross off a date on one of his stairs, climbing one step closer to where he wanted to be in his hockey career.

Many kids would balk at that kind of structure. Kelly says it was just what Connor needed. And it worked. "That's when I realized he needed things broken down. He set massive goals. He wanted to play rep hockey. He wanted to play in the OHL as a fifteen-year-old. He wanted to be drafted into the NHL. He had all these grandiose dreams."

After his final year of house league hockey ended, Connor McDavid tried out for a AAA team. He was seven years old and still one year younger than everyone else in the league. He made the team.

Brian McDavid knew hockey. Already he was seeing something that

Kelly still refused to acknowledge: that their young son was special. She never wanted to become one of those parents who believe their child is the next great one. "Let's not get excited," she told her husband. "I have seen all these kids everybody talks about all the time. Where did they go? Nowhere. I was always of the mindset, let's do this for fun. Let's not get too excited about this."

As Connor progressed to competitive hockey, other parents could see how good he was. He could fly on skates. He had a quick, powerful shot. He saw the game differently than other kids. The puck always seemed to find him, because he anticipated where it would be. Wayne Gretzky was like that, and Brian McDavid saw that same talent in his son.

Adding to his skills was an unworldly drive that was part of Connor even from a young age. He never stopped working at his game. Being good was never going to cut it; Connor McDavid wanted greatness. "He always wanted to go for it," Kelly says. "That was his focus. He was very determined, and he was going to make it no matter what."

Kelly had been spending much of her time looking after Cameron's hockey needs while Brian cared for Connor. Often, they were in different rinks on the same night. Brian was clearly excited about Connor's rare abilities. On a night off for Cameron, Kelly sat and watched Connor play and saw it—her son really was special. "I was like, 'Oh my god, did everybody see that?' I sort of had one of those 'aha' moments, like, he's really good." He was twelve years old. Kelly knew then that Connor had a real chance to live his dreams and make it in hockey.

With Brian keeping watch over Connor's hockey development, Kelly was there for everything else in his life. She knew car rides were her best opportunity to make sure her son remained grounded. "How did I help him? I just support him. That's it. I'm there for them. I support them. I'm constantly talking to him. That's all we did as we drove to and from games and practices. We just talked. It's just spending time with them and supporting them."

Cameron continued to play competitive hockey, and the McDavids made sure they were supporting both boys. "Great hands. Great skating ability," Kelly says about Cameron. "But he just didn't have the same intensity for the game that Connor does. And he had other interests. He loves music and friends, and he loved all that stuff. He's not as intense."

Cameron made noises about giving up hockey when he was seven, but he stuck it out. A few years later, he was on the verge of quitting again. He was playing on a good team, and it should have been a year of great memories. Instead, it evolved into a year they would all like to forget. "There were a couple of kids and parents on that team who were bullies," Kelly says. "The coach wasn't doing anything about it. We just told him to stand up for himself. And he did."

Kelly and Brian encouraged their older son to finish out the year and honour his commitment to the team. He did that. Kelly became that mom who attended every practice to monitor the situation. His team ended up winning an Ontario championship. A victory party followed, and Cameron had no interest in going. "I said, 'Oh, we're going to the party. And you're going to hold your head up high because you were part of that team. You go up and thank the coaches, and we're right out of there.'" Kelly was firm. They went to the victory party, and he thanked his coaches. In and out. Cameron was done with that team. The following year, he got a fresh start on a new team. His passion for hockey was back.

Connor never had to stare down bullies. Kelly says, "No, because kids wanted to be his friend. Kids wanted to be around him." For Connor, the concern was always the pressure of expectations, with much of that pressure coming from Connor himself. "When he would get quiet, I would worry," his mother says. "I think he's just a very introspective person. And when he was dealing with things and trying to work through things, he got quiet. And I was always the one, 'What's wrong? Tell me what's happening.'"

By the time Connor was twelve, there was a buzz about him around hockey rinks. Scouts came to watch him play. Agents called. Kelly says through it all Connor stayed grounded. "He doesn't like to be the centre of attention. He always deflects to his teammates."

Coaches trying to build stacked spring and summer league rosters wanted Connor on their team. Connor could play for free, the coaches told the McDavids. The coaches knew that, with Connor on their team, other top players would most certainly follow. The McDavids' answer was always no. They left the spring and summer decisions up to Connor. He chose to play on the teams that his friends played on. And the McDavids always paid.

Parents were also buzzing about Connor. And sometimes it was a nasty buzz fuelled by jealousy. For the most part, there had been no major issues in his younger years. Parents marvelled at the kid who made the game seem so effortless. But as Connor got older, Kelly noticed a different noise coming from some parents.

When he was in grade seven, Connor transferred to a private school in Toronto that caters to elite athletes and began playing in the Greater Toronto Hockey League, on a team with a pecking order already established. Some parents weren't too pleased that the young phenom was being dropped in and messing things up for their kids. Kelly says the school experience was great, but the hockey that year was challenging. "There were some parents who thought their kid was a star on the team. There were weird things going on with the parents. And they didn't like us very much either."

Complicating matters was the team's decision to bring Brian on as an assistant coach. Kelly was feeling the chill from the other parents. "'Who does he think he is?' they asked. So I just stayed in the corner and tried to be invisible."

If there were issues with Connor being so good, they often surfaced from parents from opposing teams. One time Connor was coming off the ice after dominating in one of his team's wins. In the stands, a mother from the other team was right at the glass, giving him the finger. At the time, he was eleven years old. "He was very upset and got in the car and said, 'Why did she do that?'" Kelly struggled to find an answer. "And you know, trying to explain to a child at that age that, unfortunately, some parents are very jealous. We just have to walk away."

There was never even a thought given to pulling Connor from Toronto after that terrible year. And things did get better. In 2012, in his final season of minor hockey with the Toronto Marlboros, he was named the Greater Toronto Hockey League player of the year.

By the time he was fifteen, there was no doubt that Connor McDavid was ready for the OHL. The family signed with the Orr Group, the management company headed up by Boston Bruins legend Bobby Orr. Nearly a half century earlier, Orr had travelled the same road that McDavid was now on: he was a young phenom, being touted as the next great one. Orr knew better than anyone what the McDavids were dealing with. Now he was Connor's agent.

The family applied to have Connor enter the OHL draft a year early and got approval. That year the Erie Otters, the worst team in the league, made Connor McDavid their first overall pick. He became just the third player ever to be made eligible for the draft as a fifteen-year-old.

And now he was leaving home and moving to Erie, Pennsylvania, to live in a new country and with people he didn't know. It was a lot to take in, for a young kid and for his mother. But if Connor McDavid was nervous about it, he sure hid it well. "He was the one trying to console us," Kelly remembers. "He was always the rock. For us, it was heart-wrenching. He was going to live with this family that we didn't know, in another country. It was scary. Connor was always very mature."

The billet family that cared for Connor for three seasons in Erie couldn't have been nicer. Bob and Stephanie Catalde had three kids. They were kind, caring people who had never billeted a hockey player before. After being hand-picked by the general manager of the Erie Otters, the Cataldes agreed to take on Connor McDavid. The Cataldes invited the McDavids for dinner before Connor moved in. Kelly knew right away he was joining a good family. "They were the best people. They looked after him like he was one of their own. They are still close with us."

Connor became part of the Catalde family. Before games, Bob would prepare Connor's favourite pre-game meal; grilled chicken, brown rice, and quinoa. On the home front, things were good.

The bigger challenges were on the ice. For a kid who hated to lose, playing on a losing team was a painful experience. By Christmas of Connor's first season in Erie, the head coach had been fired. It changed nothing. The losses continued.

When his mom called, Connor never opened up much about how he was dealing with all the changes in his life, but Kelly knew from experience that he would be bothered by the losses that were piling up during his first year of junior. One day she was checking her phone while in line at Starbucks and realized she had missed a call from Connor the night before. "He never called that late. I texted him that morning and said, 'Is everything okay?' He said, 'I'm homesick.' And I lost it."

It was a rare moment of vulnerability for a fifteen-year-old who had transitioned from minor hockey to major junior hockey almost seamlessly. Those goals that Connor and his mother had discussed years before? He was reaching them, one by one. And as he got better, so did his team.

In his second year of junior, Connor played for Team Canada at the World Junior Championship, becoming just the sixth sixteen-year-old to make the team. That year, the Canadian junior team did not have a good tournament. It was one of the few times Canada failed to win a medal. And it was one of the few times in his hockey career that Connor McDavid wasn't a difference-maker. He was benched for long stretches. In a key game against the Czech Republic, McDavid got the call in a game-deciding shootout. And he missed. The criticism levelled at him on social media was vicious.

"It was awful." When they pile on a kid, a mother feels it too. Kelly McDavid was hurting for her son. "People can be terrible. He's really not on social media anymore."

Connor McDavid returned to his dominating self the following season. It would be his last year of junior hockey, and it was not without drama. Just over a month before another World Junior Championship and a chance at redemption for both McDavid and Team Canada, Connor got into a rare fight. His mother was at home, watching on TV and feeling helpless: "Yeah, why did he do that?"

Kelly McDavid's worst fears were realized. Her son was injured in the fight. Connor had a broken bone in his right hand. It became touch and go to see if he would be healthy enough to compete for Canada.

"It's life lessons," Kelly told her son. "You have to learn how to get through adversity."

Brian and Kelly got Connor to a hand specialist in London, Ontario. By the time the 2015 World Juniors rolled around, he was ready. He played a starring role on a team loaded with future NHL players as Canada won gold. Connor McDavid, still just seventeen years old, was a tournament all-star.

He finished his junior career with a flourish. The Erie Otters made it to the OHL final. Even though he'd missed nearly two months of the season with his hand injury and the junior tournament, McDavid was among the league's top scorers. There was absolutely no doubt that he would be the first player taken in the 2015 NHL draft, and he would become a star in the NHL.

The Edmonton Oilers won the lottery that gave them the first pick and the opportunity to draft McDavid. He had achieved another one of the goals he had set when he was young: to be drafted first overall into the NHL.

Connor McDavid was now eighteen years old. Other kids his age were walking onto university campuses for the first time, heading off to frosh parties, and ripping into beer kegs. Connor was hanging out with men who had wives and mortgages and children. He stepped right from junior hockey to the NHL. He was playing with men now, and he still made the game look easy.

His mother watched every one of his games. She saw him rack up seventeen points in his first thirteen NHL games. And she watched in horror as he caught an edge and slammed hard into the boards in a game just a month into his rookie season. Two Philadelphia Flyers crashed into the boards with him. "It's hard to watch," Kelly says. Her son had a broken collarbone and would miss three months of hockey.

Ever since that injury, Kelly has found herself even more anxious. "I'm always at the edge of my seat. I see him racing towards the boards, I'm yelling at the TV: 'Be careful. Be careful.'"

Even though Connor McDavid is a huge star, his mom still worries, still checks in, still makes sure the pressure of greatness is manageable. They text each other often, but especially when Connor and his team are struggling. Kelly wishes she could do more to comfort him. "It's hard to watch, and talk to him, and to know that he is so frustrated. It's what I keep saying: 'I wish I could help you in some way.'"

Has it been a perfect journey for the McDavids? Of course not. In this game, Kelly came to realize early on, perfect doesn't exist. There were many missed vacations along the way, replaced by hockey trips and car rides to and from the rink. "For me, there were a lot of sacrifices. There were a lot of fights over hockey. The money we spent on equipment and tournaments when there were lots of things I wanted to do in the house. But we had to buy new skates or those kinds of things. On the schedule, we would have it free, but at the last minute, they'd schedule a practice. That, to me, was very frustrating. I have a very close family. We'd want to get together; always there were tournaments and trying to work around them."

This is as close as Kelly McDavid comes to complaining about hockey. "There are ups and downs. I know there are sacrifices to get them to the level they were at, and it was totally worth it." The game has made the family unit stronger. It has made all of their lives richer.

For Connor's older brother, Cameron, hockey was a game he played for fun. And he managed to keep it fun. He met many of his friends playing hockey. Away from the rink, he found time to play guitar. He became good enough to be accepted into a music program at Western University in London. After a year of studying music, Cameron applied for a spot at Ivey Business School at Western. He graduated on the dean's honour list. Many of the lessons he learned from playing team sports, he has found, are transferable to the business world.

Kelly says Cameron has succeeded by forging his own path in life. "He is a quiet goal-setter. He's competitive with himself and others as well in a sort of quiet way. He's outgoing. He's fun . . . He's done so well."

It's not surprising that Kelly McDavid reflects on her family's journey with some pride. Both of her boys have done well. "We have the luxury of looking back," she says. "I think everything happened the way it was supposed to happen. I think it all worked out perfectly."

Very few players come along with Connor McDavid's focus and talent. Kelly understands that. Her advice to young mothers? "Just support your kids. And enjoy the journey, because it goes by fast."

CHAPTER 2

Kids from the Desert

"Listen to their dreams, no matter how big they are, and support them in pursuing those dreams, because you never know what the future holds for them. If a kid from the desert made it to the NHL, anyone can do it."
—Ema Matthews

BILLY MATTHEWS WAS ONE of the first fans to buy into hockey in the desert. He bought season tickets, and he often brought his young nephew Auston to watch the new NHL team in Phoenix, the Coyotes. Auston would sit on Billy's lap and soak up the excitement. He loved those games with his uncle. The seed was planted.

Auston's mother, Ema, was ill-prepared for her son's love affair with hockey. She was born and raised in Mexico and knew little about the game. She fully expected that Auston's early affection for hockey would pass. But it didn't. "Auston started to let us know he wanted to play hockey. We ignored his request for a little bit. When he was four years old, we finally decided to give him some ice skating lessons. And from there, that's all he wanted to do."

Ema and her husband, Brian, enrolled Auston into the Jr. Coyotes minor hockey program when he was five years old. Ema says from that moment, her son never looked back. "Auston was just a great athlete, and we could see that at a young age. He played pretty much every sport growing up, and excelled at whatever he played. But with hockey, you could see right away that it was the one for him. Every day, he would wake up early and run straight to the garage to practise his hockey drills before school. Some days the temperature in the garage would reach a hundred and twenty degrees Fahrenheit, but that didn't stop him."

There remained a hope—almost an expectation within the family—that Auston would tire of hockey and find his way to a baseball diamond to play the sport his father excelled at. For a while, he did play baseball, and there was no doubt he had talent. He had a strong arm and was an exceptional hitter. But while he enjoyed baseball, the kid loved hockey. And his parents could see that.

Ema Matthews was now a full-on hockey mom and had to learn on the fly all the things that seem to come so naturally for many mothers. Auston was five, and Ema also had two daughters. They would all rush off to the rink together so Auston would be on time for hockey practice. "And my oldest would do her homework in the rink, and my toddler would be running around. He had practice two to three times a week, and then he had games over the weekend."

There weren't enough teams around Arizona to form leagues. So travel became a necessary part of the hockey routine. Auston often played games in Las Vegas and California. As he got older and hockey became more competitive, Brian went with him to tournaments on the east coast. The more they travelled, the more people got to see how good Auston was becoming.

The birth of NHL hockey in Arizona was paying dividends already. Auston Matthews was a natural.

ONE OF THE FIRST stars in Phoenix, and one of Auston's favourite players, was Coyotes captain Keith Tkachuk. He was a top scorer, and he was feisty. Auston liked that.

Keith had married Chantal Oster in February 1997, shortly after the Winnipeg Jets made the move to Phoenix and became the Coyotes. Chantal had grown up in Winnipeg. Now she was uprooted from her family and from the friends she had known her whole life. "A lot of people think it's glamorous. There are a lot of things along the way that are a little bit difficult."

Chantal knew what she was getting into when she chose Keith. Hockey was a big part of her life while she was growing up. Her brother, Craig, played junior hockey, then some pro hockey, before settling into law school. He is now one of the top player agents in the game. Chantal had spent plenty of time in hockey rinks before Keith came into her life.

It didn't take long for the couple to fall in love with Phoenix. They had their two boys there, first Matthew, born in 1997, and then Brady in 1999. Chantal and Keith made friends easily. The weather was awesome. And now they had two sons. Life was good.

Just when everything seemed so comfortable, it all fell apart. After nearly five full seasons in Phoenix, Keith was traded to the St. Louis Blues. "I was devastated," Chantal remembers. "We had just built a brand-new home in Arizona. I was absolutely in love with Arizona. We had all these friends. I thought our world was ending when he was traded."

Hindsight would paint a different picture. St. Louis turned out to be a perfect family fit. A third Tkachuk child, daughter Taryn, was born there. Keith spent nearly a decade playing with the Blues. When he retired in 2010, there was never any doubt that the family would make a permanent home in St. Louis.

But in 2001, there was no benefit of hindsight for the young mother whose life had just been turned upside down. "At the time, you have a three-year-old and a one-and-a-half-year-old. And as a hockey player, you get traded and you leave within twenty-four hours. And it's the wife who is left behind who is dealing with everything."

The family was busy settling into life in St. Louis when Chantal and Keith signed Matthew up for his first minor hockey team. He was about to turn four and just learning to skate. For the other parents, it was a big deal to have the son of an NHL star playing on their sons' team.

Keith's new teammates were also excited to see the next generation of Tkachuks take up hockey. In fact, one of the veterans went out to watch young Matthew play his first game. As debuts go, Chantal says, Matthew's couldn't have been much worse. "Well, Matthew was the worst on the team. He was just awful. And Doug Weight, who is a teammate of Keith's, and his entire family came to watch. It was embarrassing. We laugh about it to this day. I think all these parents thought they were getting the ringer. Instead, they literally got the worst player on the team."

There was no doubt in anyone's mind that Matthew's terrible first game was just a one-off. Both Matthew and his brother loved hockey. The game was in their genes. Chantal says from a young age, both Matthew and Brady were determined to follow in their father's footsteps. "Matthew, probably from one year old, he'd always have one of those mini sticks in his hand, and he would always be shooting balls around the house into those mini nets. So I think it was sort of embedded in them at a young age."

Because they were so close in age, if Matthew was playing hockey, Brady was too. "Brady always tried to do what his brother could do," Chantal says. "He was the smaller, younger brother for a long time. There is no question he tried to emulate his brother."

Because of their age difference, the boys played on the same team just once in their minor hockey careers, when Brady joined Matthew's novice team. "And I just remember, they all tried, the entire team tried to get Brady to score. He was little, like a little itty-bitty thing. It was really cute. And when you think of your favourite memories, this is one of them."

There is plenty of travel for NHL players, and much of the time during the hockey season, Chantal was on her own with her three children. She made it work with the help of her hockey family. "The whole thinking 'It takes a village to raise a child'—I had a great village. I had a very involved husband when he could be. I had amazing grandparents, who would do hockey trips. Other parents would help with drives to and from practices if I needed it. I think every hockey mom goes through that, where they have multiple kids playing sports. They have to divide and conquer. I was just lucky I had a lot of people that helped me out in that way."

When Keith was around, Chantal says, he was all in. "It was like my babysitter to send the boys to the rink with Keith." The family scrapbook is full of photos with Matthew and Brady posing for pictures with some of the biggest stars of the NHL—Crosby, Malkin, Ovechkin—with Matthew and Brady showing off their toothless grins.

Chantal knew hockey and could see that her two sons were quickly developing into pretty good hockey players. They could score. They were feisty. Always, they were having fun. Watch them play, and you could tell right away they were Keith's boys. "He pushed them pretty hard," Chantal says. "But he pushed them because he had confidence in what they were capable of. Keith's favourite line is 'Play better.' So the better you play, you're going to get more opportunities and be put in better situations. So it was just his way of saying 'Push yourself to be better than the next person.'"

It could be difficult at times, meeting the expectations of a father who was a star in the NHL, and Chantal realized that. "I was definitely the good cop. Keith was the bad cop. He obviously has a lot more experience in the hockey world. So he would point out more of the negatives. And I was always there to point out all the positives."

Hockey was now eating up a lot of time and attention in the Tkachuk family. There were times Chantal worried it was happening at the expense of her daughter, Taryn. "I don't want to say she got the short end of the stick, because she's very spoiled herself. But we would travel to go see the boys, and she'd be left home with a grandparent, or we would miss something of hers or whatever."

Like her brothers, Taryn was a gifted athlete. Unlike Matthew and Brady, it took time for her to find her sport. She played hockey for a few years, but it was never a passion. She moved on to soccer and became good at it. Then one day, Taryn came to her mother and said she was done with soccer. She was feeling burnt out. "And I just looked at her and had to take a breath, because I was like, 'Oh my gosh, you're so good at soccer.'" Although surprised, Chantal encouraged Taryn to find her passion in another sport. That's when Taryn became a field hockey player. She has gone on to play Division 1 at the University of Virginia. "She had a really late start to it compared to a lot of her peers, but because she loved it, she ended up excelling at it. I just think it's important to be active and have fun."

Chantal's two boys' passion never wavered. They played many sports growing up, and Chantal is convinced the variety helped them develop into better athletes. But from day one, their passion was hockey. Matthew quickly became a star on every team he played on. It was the same for Brady. "They've been fortunate," Chantal says.

While his kids were growing up, Keith's NHL career marched along. It was hardly a normal family backdrop. But it was their reality. When Keith was away, it was Chantal who tried to keep things together on the home front. "Well, I mean, I'd have to call them in often to get homework done or to come and eat, because every day after school, they'd throw on Rollerblades, and I'd have to drag them in to do what they were supposed to do."

She realized soon enough that homework was a tough sell to her two boys. "They always had their mind set on their ultimate goal. And that was being a professional hockey player. So I would say that probably trumped. For me, it was always trying to find that balance."

School work suffered because travel became so frequent as the boys played minor hockey. "Once you got to a certain level, that AAA, there are not multiple teams locally that you can play. So they'd usually be missing Friday of school and be flying out Thursday night and coming back Sunday night. So it was a real commitment."

There were tournaments in Chicago. In Dallas. In Boston and Detroit. And at times, it could be hectic. You would never hear Chantal complain. Not then, not now. "Youth hockey was really a big part of our life. It was our world. I don't feel like I've sacrificed at all. In fact, I just feel like hockey has brought a whole bunch of blessings for our family."

By the time her two boys were teenagers, there was no doubt that both Matthew and Brady Tkachuk had the talent to keep climbing, and maybe be like their dad and play in the NHL. But as Chantal and Keith understood better than most parents, some of the toughest miles on the road to get there were still to be travelled.

⁊

THE PATHS OF THE Tkachuk boys and Auston Matthews never crossed when they were all living in Arizona, but they would later on, when the boys were teenagers. The hockey world is small. And the higher you climb, the smaller it gets. Matthew Tkachuk and Auston Matthews were born just months apart in Scottsdale, Arizona. When they were sixteen years old, they finally came together as teammates with the USA Hockey National Team Development Program, based out of Detroit.

Having the Coyotes around helped grow minor hockey programs in Arizona, and Auston Matthews benefited. Auston often played in tournaments in more traditional hockey markets, and it was hard to miss him. Scouts began to marvel at the kid who had grown up in the desert and developed a game that seemed flawless.

All of the travel to tournaments took a huge slice out of the Matthews family budget, but never, Ema says, at the expense of her other children. "My oldest is a girl, and one of the ways we make her feel special is that she was our first child. She is our oldest and smartest of the three. She is the one we have the most pictures of when she was a child. Auston was our second child and the only boy, so that's special. And, of course, our youngest girl is our baby and the most spoiled. We just love our kids, and they all know it."

Only the best players in the country join the US development program. Almost every player invited has dominated minor hockey all their lives. They are brought together, and every day becomes a competition. Chantal says for Matthew first, and later for Brady, joining such an elite hockey program was an eye-opener. "You get into that situation when you're playing with a whole bunch of great athletes and you're no longer one of the best. And so, I think there were times for both of them where they experienced a little bit of adversity. But I think it just forced them to work harder and push themselves even more."

For Auston Matthews, the adversity was multiplied. He had just joined the program and wanted to prove to the coaches and to his new teammates that he belonged. But in just his second game, he collided with another player and broke his femur. His recovery took months. His mom says it was the greatest challenge he had faced in his young hockey career. "He had to have surgery, and he was in a wheelchair for two months, then on crutches. He was so disappointed, and he was scared that he wouldn't be able to play again."

He came back later that season and hardly seemed to miss a beat. Chantal, who was watching her son Matthew, kept being drawn to the kid from Arizona who seemed to do everything so well. "He stuck out as a special player the minute everyone saw him. He was under the radar in Arizona."

Auston Matthews and Matthew Tkachuk spent two seasons together. It was a tight group, and the two of them developed a strong friendship. Brady Tkachuk would join the development program after his brother and Auston Matthews had moved on. They were all on the fast track to the NHL. The question they asked was the same one asked by so many families in the same situation: What is the best road to get there? In the end, the answer was different for each player, and they ended up travelling three different roads.

Auston Matthews took the most unconventional route: he said no to US college hockey and no to major junior hockey in Canada, opting instead to play professional hockey in Switzerland. He was coached there by Marc Crawford, a Canadian who had won a Stanley Cup coaching Colorado twenty years earlier. Auston's mother, Ema, stayed with him in Switzerland. The family decision to grow Auston's game by having him play in Europe is one Ema Matthews has never regretted. "The decision was based on what we felt was best for his development. The opportunity to play there, with professional players, under Marc Crawford, who has been highly successful as an NHL coach, was an absolute gift of an opportunity for him and our family, and he learned a lot and continued a rapid pace of development."

To Chantal's chagrin, the Tkachuk boys headed in different directions. Matthew was first up. He had a full scholarship offer from the University of Notre Dame, and Chantal so badly wanted him to accept. But at her husband's urging, she backed off. Keith told her, "Listen, he has to make this decision. Because in five years, we can't have him come back and say to us, 'What if?'" Matthew Tkachuk said no to the hockey scholarship and took his talent to the OHL and the London Knights. "And it turned out he made the right decision," his mother says.

Brady's moment of truth came two years later. For most of his life, he'd followed the lead of his older brother. This time, with his parents' support, Brady headed in his own direction. He passed on the opportunity to play in the OHL and accepted a scholarship offer at Boston University. Chantal says that too became a good decision. "It just all depends on the kid and what they want to do. Because if they do what they want to do, the chances of their success are going to be better because they are taking ownership of their decision."

Matthew Tkachuk thoroughly enjoyed his one season in London. His team won a Canadian junior championship. Matthew was a star on the team. Off the ice, he bonded well with his billet family. Wayne and Sue Burke had no kids, and Matthew became close to them.

The Burkes took a southern vacation during that hockey season while Matthew was with them. Sue cut her foot while they were away, and the cut became infected. Antibiotics did nothing to help. The infection got worse, and it spread. Matthew's billet mom ended up dying from what had seemed a simple infection. Chantal says her son was absolutely crushed. "The only other loss Matthew had experienced was my mom, his grandma. He was close to this woman. It was a really difficult time." Chantal flew to London to be with Matthew. She took him to the hospital so he could pay his last respects. At his billet mom's funeral, Matthew was a pallbearer. "It was really, really hard. I don't even know how you prepare a child for that. Any time your child is suffering, it's hard."

The London Knights dedicated their championship season to Sue Burke. Matthew devoted himself to making her proud.

Matthew and his friend Auston Matthews were reunited in June 2016 at the NHL Entry Draft in Buffalo. By now, it was clear they were both going to be stars in the NHL. The draft was a stepping stone to getting there.

Ema Matthews was in Buffalo as her son was chosen first in the draft by the Toronto Maple Leafs. A kid from a non-traditional hockey market was now going to the hottest hockey market on the planet. As Auston's name was called, his mother was overwhelmed with emotion. "I saw him walk on the stage, and I could see all his childhood dreams come true."

Matthew Tkachuk was taken sixth overall by the Calgary Flames. The two friends from the US development program stepped right into the NHL and seemed at home there. By the end of his first NHL game, Auston Matthews had scored four goals.

Two years later, it was Brady Tkachuk's turn. He was selected fourth overall by the Ottawa Senators. He stayed just one year at Boston University. Now he was playing in the NHL right out of the draft.

Auston, Matthew, and Brady. All three of them born in Arizona. Now making millions. And among the biggest stars in the league.

Ema Matthews, the novice hockey mom when she began her run in the sport, is so much wiser now. She had no idea that those trips to the rink with Brian's brother Billy would light the spark to produce one of the best players in hockey. "I don't believe he has reached his peak now. There are always things to get better at, new challenges, new things to conquer. Auston was always very motivated to be the best, to try new things, to venture into the unknown."

Chantal Oster-Tkachuk was better prepared for what the hockey world might throw at her. As she watched her kids develop, she could see they had a chance. "They knew from a very young age. They were like 'Oh, we're going to be professional hockey players.' As they climbed the ladder throughout their youth careers and then got into the US development program, it started becoming more of a reality that it could be possible. Then it came to just elevating their games to the highest level. I think the kids who quit are the ones who probably don't have the same kind of drive and passion for it. Because if they had the drive and passion, they wouldn't quit, right?"

Quitting was never on the radar for the Tkachuk boys or for Auston Matthews. Nor was it ever on the radar for their mothers, who did so much to support their hockey journeys. "Parents always make sacrifices for their kids; it is part of being a parent," Ema Matthews believes. "I don't know if we would have done anything differently. Each struggle and success was a learning experience for us as parents and as a family."

Chantal sees sport as the great family unifier. One of her proudest moments as a mother was in 2020 when the NHL was shut down by COVID. The boys were home and able to cheer on their sister, Taryn, in her final year of high school field hockey as she went on to win a state championship. "It was really fun to make her the centre of attention for once, because I think the boys steal a lot of the limelight in the family. And I think it was just really special that they got to support her."

Her boys turned out alright, she says, as hockey players and as people. "Both boys had a passion for the game. My role was to support that. And I did that to the best of my ability. But I mean, I like to think that they're good human beings too, which, to me, is more important than being good players. And especially as they get more involved in this professional life that they always stay true to their roots and grounded."

Ema Matthews says the role of the hockey mom is pretty simple: to be there for your kids. You never know where the journey will lead. "Listen to their dreams, no matter how big they are, and support them in pursuing those dreams, because you never know what the future holds for them. If a kid from the desert made it to the NHL, anyone can do it."

CHAPTER 3

Sacrifice and Chance

"I don't know how many times I woke up and said, 'How are we going to do this? How are we going to get through this week?' That was the worst thing. It was a strain on me every single day. We just had to find a way to make it work."
—Terri Konecny

WHEN RHONDA HENLEY GAVE birth to her only child, Troy, in 1997, she had no doubt that Troy's sporting life would be played out on a football field. Her husband, Troy Sr., or Big Troy as she calls him, played some semi-pro football, and she was convinced that Little Troy would follow in his dad's footsteps. "There's no Henley that don't play football" was Rhonda's way of thinking.

Troy was born in Philadelphia. He was four years old when Rhonda and Troy Sr. signed him up for his first football team. Little Troy was big and athletic and talented. It should have been a perfect fit. But

Little Troy hated it. "He finally got into the car, and he said, 'Mom, I don't want to play football. I just don't want to play anymore.'" Just like that, Rhonda says, Troy's football career was over.

The Henleys saw value in sports and quickly enrolled Troy in soccer and baseball, hoping he would find his game and run with it. He enjoyed soccer well enough but had no passion for it. Baseball was the same: he had all kinds of talent, but he found the game way too slow. So his mom and dad kept looking for a fit.

As it turns out, Little Troy's sport was staring him in the face. It just took some time for his parents to realize it. Between his soccer games and his baseball practices, Troy was out on the street playing ball hockey with neighbourhood kids. Even though they were living in a city that was home to the NHL's Philadelphia Flyers, hockey was never on Rhonda's radar. "I didn't even know what a blue line was." But Troy loved his road hockey games, and Rhonda was thrilled when her son came to her and said he wanted to be a hockey player. Sports were important to the Henleys, and they were willing to make it work.

Soon Troy had his first pair of skates. Veteran hockey moms know there is a trick to skate sizing: go a size smaller than shoe size. Rhonda Henley was far from being a veteran. "I ended up getting skates that were too big, and he flopped around like a newborn baby calf on the ice."

Rhonda enrolled Troy in a learn-to-skate program called Snowplow Sam. It was her first real experience with a sport that was about to consume her life. "The instructor basically told me to walk him to the door and just walk away. I remember thinking, 'How is he going to get where all the other kids are?' He just held onto the boards all the way to the other kids."

Troy Henley was six years old when he skated for the first time. It was a late start for a kid who still had so much to learn about his new sport. Skating? Offsides? Icing? He knew nothing about any of it. But he wanted to learn, and he wanted to be good. So together Troy and Rhonda set out on their hockey journey. They were two rookies, a mother and her son, who were about to become hockey experts.

As Troy Henley was learning the basics of hockey, folks in rural southern Ontario were already raving about a kid who seemed like a natural. Travis Konecny was raised in Clachan, about forty-five minutes southwest of London. There was hunting and fishing. And there was hockey. The Konecnys fit right in. Travis's father, Rob, played Junior B hockey as a teenager. His mother, Terri, grew up in a hockey family and played for a few years. "We knew hockey," she says matter-of-factly.

Their first child, Chase, came along in 1995, and Travis was born eighteen months later. Because they were so close in age, they were often teammates early on. Chase and Travis were both good players. But Terri says you could tell there was something special about Travis. "The puck seemed to just follow him around. But I never took it for granted that he was a good hockey player."

Travis Konecny had been playing hockey just a few years when a coach approached Terri and Rob, asking if Travis would be interested in playing on an elite summer team. He would be playing with older kids in Brantford, Ontario, about an hour and a half from home. For the first time in his life, he would be playing without his older brother on his team. Terri and Rob saw it as an amazing opportunity, a chance for Travis to test his skills and grow his game with top players from another part of the province. But Travis wanted no part of it. "He did not want to go," Terri says. "Actually, it was funny. He did not want to play unless his brother was playing with him."

They drove to Brantford for Travis's first tournament, with Terri's mother along for the ride. Travis's grandmother made sure he didn't back out. "She would open the door and say, 'Going, Trav?' He'd say 'No.' She kind of shoved him in, shut the door, and said, 'Let's go, we're going to Brantford.'" Terri laughs as she remembers that trip. "She was so funny. She shoved him in the car, because she loves hockey. She wanted to go."

The drive to Brantford wasn't pretty. Terri says there were plenty of tears from Travis. "He did not want to go on the ice. Anyway, he went on. He did really well. He came off the ice and said to my husband, 'It was so much fun. Can I come back next week?' That's kind of how it started. From there, we went off to AAA, and that's how hockey started for him."

For Terri, it was a valuable lesson in parenting. Although it was hard watching Travis so unhappy about playing with a new team, "Sometimes, you just have to challenge them a bit," she says.

FROM THE FIRST TIME he put on a pair of skates, there was little doubt that Troy Henley had found his passion. He loved skating, and every week saw a vast improvement. Rhonda remembers the time she missed one of Troy's skating lessons. Her husband was there with a video camera. "He says, 'You gotta see this.' And I'm thinking, 'Oh my gosh, don't tell me he fell or something like that. Sure enough, he was skating backwards. And I said, 'Oh my god, I can't believe he picked that up.' And we just couldn't believe it. And then he started flying the next day."

Troy was raw, of course. And the rules and nuances of hockey were still an adventure. But Rhonda says he was getting it. "It took him a bit to catch up with some of the techniques, like how to stop or the proper way to get up if you fell on the ice. But he was a natural."

Troy hadn't been playing very long when he was picked up by a AA team. Rhonda says it was more competitive than a house league, but still a long way from the high-level hockey he would soon be playing. "A lot of kids ended up joining. There were no Travis Konecnys. They were pretty much kids that just wanted to play and get a feel for a little bit of travel hockey. And I had him there, and that's when Troy actually took off."

The more Troy played, the more he loved it and the better he got. The more he played, the more expensive hockey became. Troy needed new sticks. He was big and quickly outgrowing his skates and equipment. There were skills development courses and more skating lessons. And now there was travel in the mix. Rhonda says hockey was putting her family in the poorhouse. "It actually was so expensive that we ended up selling our house in Philadelphia because we had a mortgage. And that's when we crossed the bridge to New Jersey."

By moving to Paulsboro, New Jersey, where homes were far less expensive, Rhonda and her family were mortgage-free. There was more cash now to keep Troy in hockey. "It was so bad. I mean, my husband was diving into his retirement fund. But I never told Troy, 'You know, dude, we just can't afford hockey.' Regardless of the cost, we were going to make it happen."

Pretty quickly Troy was making a name for himself. He was a big, steady defenceman who knew how to use his size to his advantage. Before long, he was playing AAA hockey and travelling all over the place to games and tournaments.

The move to New Jersey provided some relief on the money front. But it didn't solve all of the family's problems because the hockey expenses kept growing. Troy would break a stick, and then what? Rhonda had no answers. "Everyone could pretty much see that Troy was using the same cracked stick," she says. "And we would tape up the blade really good so that nobody knew there was a crack until he went to go take a slapshot and the puck didn't go anywhere. That's pretty much when people knew, okay, maybe the stick has a crack in it. And I didn't know the sport well enough to know that people would pick up on things like that."

Others at the rink could see that the Henleys were struggling financially and stepped up to help. Sometimes a parent would quietly hand Troy a new stick. One of Troy's coaches, former NHL forward Keith Primeau, passed on a few pairs of used skates. Even then, it wasn't enough.

One time when money was really tight, Rhonda and Troy crossed the bridge and headed back to Philadelphia. They found a busy street corner and asked for help from strangers. "There is a place in northeast Philadelphia called Five Points. And it's like five directions. You know, you could go in five different directions if you came to this stoplight. And I had suited up Troy with his jersey. And it was cold. And we had a bucket and his hockey stick. And we went with another mom on the team with her son. Just the two moms and two boys. And we tried to raise money for a tournament. There was just no way we could afford it. And all we could do is suit the kids up and try to ask for money. And by the time the day was over, we had maybe a couple of hundred dollars. And we split it between Troy and the other kid on his team."

It was difficult, Rhonda says, asking for money from strangers. "We've never had to do that. Ever. Like for anything. I mean, we would always manage."

The money issues were hard enough, but there were other challenges. Troy was one of the few Black players in a game that's still predominantly white. He faced racism. "He heard 'Go back to the jungle,'" his mother says. "They would say, 'Why are you playing this sport? You should be playing basketball.'"

While his teammates offered support, the racial taunts kept coming from players from opposing teams. His mother says Troy tried to control his anger. Often, it was just impossible. "He would actually warn them first. And then they would keep talking, and that's when Troy would end up fighting them on the ice. I would just tell Troy, 'You know, I could understand how angry you are.'"

Walking away from hockey was never an option. The Henleys weren't quitters. Despite the ugliness that crept into their lives from time to time, Troy still loved hockey. And Rhonda loved going to the rink and watching Troy develop into a solid hockey prospect.

The kid who learned to skate at age six was a budding star just four years later. His size and his physical game were impressive. He blocked shots without fear. If a teammate was in trouble, Troy was there for him. He was really a perfect tough-as-nails defenceman. Somehow, those nasty racist comments only made him tougher to play against.

Troy Henley was twelve years old when he started working with an agent, whom Rhonda met one day at the hockey rink. "I was there by myself. A gentleman walked over and said he was looking for Troy's mother, and I'm already thinking, 'Oh my god, do I owe this guy money?'" Troy was young for an agent, but for a family unfamiliar with hockey, it was difficult to figure out the right path to follow. There were no contracts to be negotiated at that age. There was no free agency. Rhonda liked the idea of bringing someone on board who knew the ins and outs of hockey. She needed help. So she retained the agent

As Troy moved into his teen years, he played in a AAA league that included several future NHL players. He more than held his own. The agent believed the time was right for Troy to move to Canada, to accelerate his progress and improve his chances of making it in hockey. His mother needed convincing. "I was a little hesitant because I'm thinking, 'Well, I've never been to Canada.' And I wasn't just going to leave him in Canada."

Rhonda held off until Troy was fourteen. Money was still tight, but Rhonda and Troy packed up and moved north. They got an apartment together in Oakville, Ontario. The agent helped Troy become part of the powerful Oakville Rangers AAA team. Rhonda was all in. If this was the best road to the NHL for Troy, they would travel it.

There were no regrets at all about leaving New Jersey and setting up shop in Canada. Junior scouts were at all of Troy's games. His team won an Ontario championship, and Troy was a big reason why they won. In just a few short years, Troy Henley grew from a big kid who looked like Bambi on skates to a young man who was one of the top defencemen of his age group. As he stood on the cusp of the 2013 OHL draft, there was absolutely no doubt that he'd found his sport.

TRAVIS KONECNY WAS PLAYING just as well as he approached the same junior draft year. But his journey to that point was completely different from Troy Henley's. When your mom and dad were hockey players and you're on skates not long after you learn to walk, it is a huge advantage. Travis made the most of it. He stood out right from the start. As he progressed through minor hockey, nothing really changed. Good from the beginning, he just kept getting better. In so many ways he was the perfect teammate, the guy who made every team he played on better. "He was always a natural leader," his mother says. "That really helped him out. He's got a good, kind heart. He makes everyone feel at ease."

There were so many differences in the upbringing of the two future teammates. They were from different countries and of different races. Travis is a rural kid; Troy, from a big city. Yet scratch the surface and you see so many similarities, including, Terri Konecny says, the financial struggles forced on them by hockey. "I don't know how many times

I woke up and said, 'How are we going to do this? How are we going to get through this week?' That was the worst thing. It was a strain on me every single day. We just had to find a way to make it work."

There were times when money was so tight that going to a restaurant, or even a grocery store, wasn't really an option. "We are a hunting family. We ate a lot of venison, lots of wild meat. We battled our way through. You just find a way."

Rob Konecny found himself out of work a few times in those years. That stereotype of hockey being a game for rich families? Terri Konecny was having none of it. "I remember there was this one article basically saying we were this rich family. I was so upset. You have no idea what I am going through. I am buying used clothing all the time. It so irritated me." It was worth it, she says, because hockey made it worth it.

Terri worked with students with special needs at a local school. When her school day ended, it was game on; she was on the run. "It was a lot of me driving from work, picking up Travis and Chase at school, having supper that was prepared the night before, because you've got to, you haven't got time to go home. That's really what it was. Everyday mom stuff."

The hockey rink was her happy place. She loved the game and the people who were drawn to it. Yet as good as Travis was at a young age, he still experienced the sting of being cut from a team that, based on skill, he probably should have made. "It was like, okay. We saw a bit of politics right away. Let's get out of here and move them on."

They moved their two boys to a neighbouring league, where Travis made the competitive team and had a great year. He changed leagues again before his minor hockey career was over, always to help his game grow, and it always meant more travel and more sacrifice for the family. The higher he climbed in the minor hockey world, the greater the family commitment. Terri says there was "a lot of running around. And planning. For AAA, a lot of times, it was four to seven nights a week. I'd get home late. Then you'd start the whole cycle over again because my husband was going back to school. I was coming home and doing the laundry. Constantly, constantly going. And there was no time for anything else."

Chase also played sports—first hockey and eventually track and field—adding to the amount on Terri's plate. "Chase had to sacrifice a lot. It was important for us to do everything possible to try to make him feel equal. Does that sound right? We never wanted to make him feel less important in the family. We felt bad for Chase. He is the quieter one too. We always worry about that. He's also Travis's biggest fan. By far."

IN THE SPRING OF 2013, Travis Konecny's and Troy Henley's lives came together. There was plenty of buzz about this draft because, yet again, a fifteen-year-old had been granted exceptional status. This time, it was a defenceman named Sean Day who entered the draft one year early.

The Ottawa 67's, who held the first overall pick, had a fierce internal debate about drafting the best fifteen-year-old in the country. In the end, they took a pass and drafted Travis Konecny. It was a bold decision that the team would never regret.

Travis Konecny was sixteen years old and moving to Ottawa. At the same time, Chase was ready to start his next chapter in life as an environmental engineering student at the University of Waterloo. Just like that, the Konecnys became empty nesters. "They both left," Terri says. "We were bored, because everything was hockey."

Ottawa also had the top pick in the second round. They were shocked to see that Troy Henley was still available. They scooped him up and figured they had a steal.

"And I'm thinking, I don't even know where Ottawa is." Rhonda Henley pulled out a map and went to work. It still wasn't time for her to let go. While Troy moved in with a billet family in his new city, Rhonda set up shop in Ogdensburg, New York, a tiny town along the Canada–US border, about an hour south of Ottawa. "I wanted to be as close as I could. So, the first thing I did was google the closest American city to Ottawa. And Ogdensburg came up. I've never been there and never heard of it. I didn't even know if I'd find a place to live there. But I was determined to be as close to Troy as I could."

Rhonda landed a job as a fitness trainer in Ogdensburg. During Troy's first season of junior hockey, she hardly missed a game. "I would drive up to the border patrol, and you know, a couple of times the border agents would say, 'How did he do?' Sometimes they didn't even ask for my passport."

For all the time Rhonda was spending with Troy, there was no indication that the wheels were about to come flying off and a promising hockey career would come crashing to a halt. His first year in Ottawa was as good a rookie season as a mother could have imagined. "Troy did phenomenal as a sixteen-year-old. He literally did fantastic. He is so big, he almost had a point to prove, that I can hang here. I'm not gonna let a puck go by. I'm not going to give up the puck. He lived that way every day."

Travis Konecny's rookie season was even better. He was Ottawa's leading scorer and by far his team's best player. And he was still only sixteen. Terri Konecny says she and Rob wore out a path to Ottawa that first season. When Travis had a game, more times than not, they were there for him. "It was really hard, to be honest, that first year. He was only sixteen. Ottawa was eight hours away. We tried to have a phone conversation about whatever it was; it could be everyday stuff. It was hard over the phone. Can't get a good vibe about how he is feeling, or if he's upset or anything, right? We really struggled with that."

Troy and Travis were the only two sixteen-year-olds on their team that season. They were far from home and dealing with all the pressure that comes with junior hockey. Travis, the scorer; Troy, the protector. Rhonda Henley says they found something in each other that got them through that first season. "They shared moments like they were brothers."

Even the racism that had seemed to dog Troy Henley most of his hockey life was no longer an issue. "He went to Canada and it stopped," Rhonda says. "That first year in Ottawa couldn't have gone much better."

Everything changed in year two. A new coach came in, and Troy Henley never was able to gain his trust. "That was probably Troy's demise," Rhonda says. "The new coach was more for playing the older players. And again, because Konecny was the first overall pick, you're not going to sit him." Most nights, Troy Henley wasn't even dressed. When he played, he was nervous and made mistakes.

Eventually, the 67's dealt Troy to a new team to give him a fresh start. He was now a member of the Saginaw Spirit. "So Troy ends up getting traded in the middle of the season," his mother says. "And all the players that were there were determined that Troy wasn't going to take their spot. So Troy wasn't gonna take their spot. And now depression starts to kick in. It was just awful. It was probably the worst time for me as a mom."

The NHL draft still provided hope. While Troy Henley was no longer a hot prospect, his name was still popping up on pre-draft scouting reports. "We were actually almost positive that he was going to make it," Rhonda says. "I mean, my whole family and friends and neighbours and everybody, they even screenshotted it when they saw Troy made the NHL draft list. People couldn't believe it, and that boosted up his spirit like, 'Oh my gosh, I can't believe it. Like I learned how to play hockey from nobody. And I'm on the NHL draft list. This is all I want in life. I want nothing else.'"

THE 2015 NHL DRAFT was full of players who were clearly going to be NHL stars: Connor McDavid, Jack Eichel, Mitch Marner. Scouts were certain Travis Konecny would become an NHL star too. Not long before, Troy Henley might have been part of the same conversation. Now there were far too many questions about a career that had stalled so suddenly.

Rhonda knew that Troy's rankings were dropping, but she never imagined how much. "I mean, we had plans on going to the draft, and it wasn't until our agent told us, 'You know, listen, don't drive down. Don't send Troy down. Just stay home.'" It was advice that would save Troy from the pain and frustration of driving to Florida and finding out there were no NHL teams interested.

As expected, Connor McDavid went first overall. Jack Eichel and Mitch Marner, a couple of other future stars, went second and fourth. Travis Konecny went twenty-fourth overall and became a first-round pick of the Philadelphia Flyers.

Rhonda and Troy watched the draft from their home in Paulsboro, New Jersey. Troy Henley's name never got called. "I remember Troy sitting back and saying, 'Mom, just turn it off.'" It was heart-wrenching. "It took the wind out of everybody's sails. It was just very hard."

It was a disappointment, Rhonda says, for many people in the town of Paulsboro. They had followed Troy's story and supported him financially when they could. "I think it was even harder because we had so many people in our corner."

Travis and Troy had been teammates, had shared the same dream. But on draft day, there was Travis Konecny, doing interviews and posing for pictures, drafted by the team in Troy's backyard. And there was Troy Henley, back home, watching.

There was nothing Travis could do to help his former teammate. He just kept playing and developing into the player many believed he could be. His final year of junior hockey did have its challenges. The year after Troy was traded, Travis struggled in Ottawa. "Maybe two or three times he called upset about something that happened, or something the coach had done, and we knew he had to battle through it," his mom says. "We constantly said, 'Remember, stay strong. Stay tough and work your way through it.'" Eventually, Travis was traded to the Sarnia Sting. "In hindsight, it made him stronger" is a mother's take on a tough stretch in her son's life.

Troy Henley's career never did recover from that awful season. He was traded around the OHL for a few seasons, then played in the Southern Professional Hockey League for a few years. And just like that, at age twenty-two, he was done with hockey. "I think people really don't know his story," Rhonda says. "They don't know about his dedication and his loyalty to the game itself. He wasn't brought up in a neighbourhood where all the kids were playing hockey."

The former teammates have lost contact, which isn't unusual in hockey. Travis Konecny is a top player in the NHL. Troy Henley is now in university and hoping someday to become a US marshal. Dreams can change.

Both families sacrificed. Both moms say if they had to do it again, they wouldn't change a thing.

"Have fun with it" is Terri Konecny's advice to other moms. "Go to the arena, enjoy it. Make friends." Some of the moms Terri met at the rink became her friends for life. "I hear all these horror stories about terrible parents, terrible kids, and I think, 'Wow, am I ever glad we didn't have that.' I enjoy going to the arena. We were hanging out with our friends every day. It was awesome."

Rhonda Henley did all she could to give Troy every opportunity to succeed. And she watched him put in so much hard work to make it happen. "I can honestly say I don't regret anything because Troy doesn't regret anything." There are no guarantees in sports, she has learned. You sacrifice. You put in the work. You hope. And you keep working. "I would like for every mom to know to stick by your player. I'm always encouraging him to keep going. Don't be discouraged. And just remind them that they're worth it."

CHAPTER 4

Slow Dance

"The boys said they actually had a lot of fun with the moms because
we weren't on them like, 'You have to get a goal. You have to score.'
We were there just to drink the wine and visit with each other."
—Kristen Crouse

LIKE ALMOST EVERY OTHER NHL team, every year the Arizona Coyotes host the fathers of their players on a road trip. The dads travel on the team charter, room with their sons on the road, share meals with the team. The full NHL experience, as a way to thank dads for all they have done to help their sons make it.

A few teams, including the Coyotes, are now hosting similar trips for the mothers. For Kristen Crouse, that mothers' trip in 2019 created memories that can still turn a crappy day into a good day. The type of memories you reach back for when you need a reminder that life can be special.

One memory in particular always puts a smile in Kristen's heart. It happened in a karaoke bar in San Jose. All of the moms had hit it off instantly. They'd travelled the same road with their sons. They'd watched them push themselves and put in the work to reach the top level of hockey. They'd wiped away tears. They'd encouraged their sons. They'd driven thousands of kilometres to and from rinks. And now, six of them were together, having drinks and sharing their stories. It was one of those nights you could never script. But somehow, it seemed to unfold so perfectly.

The karaoke part of the night was over, and one of the players tipped the DJ and got him to play some eighties dance tunes for the moms. It was the music the women had danced to when they were young and out on the town. On this night, the six moms were dancing with their now adult sons. Back-to-back retro music. They were having a blast.

And then, somehow, it got even better. A slow song came on.

If their boys had still been teenagers, you can just imagine how awkward this could have been. But now they were older, more mature, and had the confidence that comes with being an NHL player. It turned into a tender moment that Kristen will remember forever. She and her son, Lawson, along with the other mothers and their sons, stayed on the floor when that slow song came on. And they slow danced.

Kristen could see others in the bar watching. "And I guess at one point a girl in the bar said, 'Like, what is going on here? How are these old ladies getting these cute young boys?'"

Beautiful.

The perks of being a hockey mom after all those years of sacrifice. "Those are fun memories. I really had a lot of fun on that moms' trip because it was just Lawson and me. We have a lot of fun when we are together."

KRISTEN'S OLDEST CHILD, SARA, was the first in the family to get the hockey bug. She was four when she began playing minor hockey in London, Ontario, about a half-hour drive from their home in Mount Brydges. Kyla, the middle child, began in gymnastics and moved into hockey later. Lawson, the youngest, played as soon as he was old enough to join a minor hockey program.

Lawson's father, Mike, kept a scrapbook from Lawson's early days in hockey. "Mike would write down the number of goals," Kristen says. "Lawson would get two goals. Three goals. Five goals. And he's a defenceman. That was a long time ago. It's like, he's got a little bit of skill here. But I thought, 'He's going to fall. Other kids are going to match him at some point.'"

Mike was right: Lawson had talent. He was big and skilled and always pushed himself to be better. Soon he was being recruited to play on an elite summer team. Remember the team Travis Konecny joined, kicking and screaming all the way to the rink? That team. Lawson and Travis have been best friends ever since.

Mike had played hockey when he was a kid, and he coached minor hockey as an adult. It was Mike who took the lead when it came to Lawson's minor hockey career. He was the one pushing and offering criticism and advice, while Kristen stayed out of it. "When they reach a certain age, they know when they did something wrong. Even to this day with Lawson's game, I just say, 'Great game.' I tried not to talk about hockey too much. I think it's important they're not inundated with hockey. I was more about school."

Kristen worked full-time as a teacher. She also looked after her daughters' sports commitments while Mike took care of Lawson's. "I look back on those days, and sometimes, with three of them, I was never home. I'm seven days a week travelling. My one daughter, her games were in Ottawa and Kingston and Sudbury. It was crazy. Now I look back and I think, 'Oh god, I don't know how I ever did that. I remember some days I'd go to work and I just wanted to cry. I just thought, 'I don't know if I can keep this up.' But you do. You just have to. Because you're doing it for your kids."

Lawson Crouse was sixteen years old when he joined the OHL as a first-round draft pick of the Kingston Frontenacs. That same year, Kyla also moved to Kingston to study and play hockey at Queen's University. Sara had already left home. Overnight, Kristen and Mike Crouse were alone together in a house with no kids. Kristen found it tough. "It was terrible. Because that meant I was an empty nester. They left at the same time. And that's the thing. Life was so, so busy, and I kept thinking, 'Oh, I can't wait till this is all done.' And then, all of a sudden, it stopped. And it's like, 'Oh my god, what do I do now?'"

Kristen and Mike's marriage didn't survive the sudden change in their lives. "To be honest, because you're so busy, you don't see each other. You don't know what's going on. So then, once the kids were all done and we were empty nesters, it was just like, 'What do we talk about now?' Our whole life was running around with our kids."

She continued to be a hockey mom. But now she was running to rinks in Kingston. She'd catch Lawson's game Friday night, Kyla's on Saturday, then head back home.

Kyla spent four seasons at Queen's. After her last game in 2017, she hung up her skates. Her mom says she hasn't played since. "Recently, I kind of said, 'How come you don't play women's pickup hockey, like just some fun stuff?' And she said, 'I don't even want to play hockey again.' Like she's done. I don't know why."

Sara played pickup as an adult for a few years, but she too is done with hockey.

Lawson's career kept going. He played for Canada twice at the World Junior Championship, winning gold in 2015 with Connor McDavid as a teammate. Five months later, he was a first-round draft pick of the Florida Panthers.

Kristen watched as her son rose to the cusp of the NHL with hardly a setback. Then, just a year after being drafted, and before he had even played a game in the NHL, Lawson was traded from Florida to Arizona. He was just nineteen years old when he played his first full season with the Coyotes.

The following season, after just eleven games, Lawson was sent to the minors and spent the rest of the year playing for the Tucson Roadrunners of the AHL. When the season ended, Kristen had her son talk to her students about his life in professional hockey. He had visited a few times over the years. That spring, after a year of setbacks, Kristen remembers that Lawson's tone was different. "He described that year as a 'punch in the gut.' He talked about the life lessons he learned thinking he made it but realizing he hadn't. It was really good for my students to hear 'Just continue to persevere.' He wanted to show his coaches that he could do it. He got better and he just developed. And so he was back in Arizona the following year."

Other than the time he spent in the minors in year two, Lawson Crouse has played for the Arizona Coyotes. His mother travels to games when she can. When she can't be there, she watches on television. "I do get nervous. And he'll fight if he has to for a teammate. So I hate fighting. There was a slip he made one game, where he went right into the wall with his back and neck. And that was a little scary, because I was watching that live. And he was out for a second. But then he got up. It's just at that point I thought, 'Oh my gosh.' As a mother, when would I find out what happened to him? Do they have automatic numbers to us? And what would I do if I needed to get there quickly? So yeah, there are times when I get really nervous because it's a sport where you could get hurt."

Over the years, she has seen so much good come from the game of hockey. She has seen her kids learn about teamwork and commitment and the benefits of hard work. She has also dealt with coaches who really shouldn't have been coaching kids, hurling abuse at young players who messed up. "How does that motivate people?" she asks. "How does that motivate children? Or anybody?"

And always, there were concerns about the cost of hockey. She was constantly looking for ways to save money. One time she and Lawson travelled to a tournament in Toronto. Lawson played on a Saturday night. If he had lost, his team would have been out, and the plan was to drive back home. But Lawson's team won, and now, late at night, Kristen went searching for an affordable hotel. They landed at a place near the airport. "I said, 'I just need a place to rest our heads.'" There was a room available. They would be setting their alarm for six the next morning to get ready for the championship game. "And I said, 'Do I have to pay full price? Because, really, I'm only going to be there six hours.' So he was kind. He actually gave it to us for half price. But I still remember Lawson and I just sort of laughing about that. I guess he saw me trying to get a deal for us. We just had a really nice time together. Because I hardly ever went to any of his games. So for us, just being together and having that time together, that was fun."

She and Lawson often talk about the journey, and all the work and sacrifice it took to get him to the NHL. As her son gets older and more reflective, Kristen says he gets it. "Lawson mentioned to his girlfriend the other day that I relied on a Crock-Pot. He said, 'I can't believe how my mom actually had meals ready for us after school, right before we had to go to a game or practice.' He said he took it for granted that it was there."

The Crock-Pots. The long rides. Drinking wine with other moms on hockey road trips. The mothers of the Coyotes players talked about all of these things during their moms' trip together. That trip, Kristen says, was perfect in so many ways. "The boys said they actually had a lot of fun with the moms because we weren't on them like, 'You have to get a goal. You have to score.' We were there just to drink the wine and visit with each other."

As they bonded, the mothers realized how similar their lives had been in many ways. "We talked about how you miss holidays. You were away. Or it's tryouts. Or the end of the season, and there are tournaments. You try to explain to family members, they say, 'Oh, they're not going to make it to the NHL, so you can skip some things.' It was kind of neat talking to other mothers about how you planned your life around hockey."

And they talked about what they were learning on the trip with their sons. They saw all the work that went into playing in the NHL, and the unrelenting pressure. "Everyone thinks it's fabulous, spectacular," Kristen says. "You're a hockey player, a superstar for all these little kids. But it can be a hard life."

Every mother, she says, left the trip filled with pride and wrought with worries. "Moms are moms. And these are our sons. We all look at them as our little boys."

CHAPTER 5

A Mom's Off-Ice Development

"If my kid came to me today and said, 'Mom, I want to go to hockey camp this summer,' I'd be 'Great. Let's do it.' I would support them a thousand percent in hockey, no matter what. I would still be that crazy hockey mom. I'm just not going to scream and yell at you on the ice."
—Tabatha Leonard

TABATHA LEONARD AND HER husband, Gord, have been together since high school in Madoc, a couple of hours east of Toronto. As happens in small towns, they got married and had children and raised two boys together. And both boys were young when they found their way to the hockey rink. That's where Tabatha's story goes a little off track. The person she became at the rink back then is not who she is today. Tabatha shares her story knowing full well she is not alone in caring too much and wanting too much from the game of hockey.

Tabatha wasn't born into the game. Her dad played in men's leagues. Every once in a while, she would get dragged to the rink to watch when she was a kid. Gord played a bit of hockey too, and back in their early days together, Tabatha would go and cheer him on. Back then, she was almost a reluctant hockey fan. "I was never like, 'Oh my god, I have to go to the arena and watch my boyfriend play hockey.' No, I couldn't care less. I didn't know the rules."

Tabatha would learn the rules and more soon enough. And she would care. Man, would she care. About everything. What changed was the birth of Tabatha and Gord's first son, Karsten. Just a few years after he learned to walk, Karsten was on the ice for the first time, and then, not long after, he was playing on his first hockey team. Tabatha never missed a game or a practice. "Because that's where you should be, because you're the mom and you need to watch the kids do everything. So even if it was him reading a book in front of the class and the teacher might have invited you, you went. You just did it, because you're the mom, and you need to go watch your kids do things and support them."

Even then, in those early days, Tabatha could see how hockey could become too much. "You put on the boots. You put on stuff and put them in their car seat, and you take them to the arena, and they fall asleep halfway there. And it was just like, all this is ridiculous." It might have been a good time to pull back a bit on hockey. Instead, Tabatha and Gord went full speed with Karsten. Their son was enjoying hockey. Tabatha and Gord were too. Really, was there any need to slow down?

Karsten turned out to be a good hockey player. Really good, actually. And one day, when he was really young, he suggested to his mom that maybe someday he would play in the NHL. Of course, many kids say the same thing. But for Tabatha, the seed was planted. "It's just like, when your kids have a passion, you help with that passion. If your kid came to you and said, 'I want to be a doctor,' well, then you're going to do everything for your kid to be a doctor. Well, my kid wanted to play in the NHL. So I'll try to do anything I can to get you to the NHL."

That dream from a young boy—to play in the NHL—changed everything for Tabatha Leonard. "I was like, 'Okay, you're pretty good. Let's see where we can take you. Let's put all of our time and effort and money and everything into hockey. Let's do it.'" Because that's what so many hockey parents do.

At first, Tabatha and Gord tried to maintain balance in Karsten's life. Yes, there were spring leagues and summer camps, the same as for so many other kids. But Karsten was encouraged to play other sports, including baseball, in the summer. Tabatha believed a break from hockey was important. A reset. And maybe a chance for Karsten to develop other skills.

And then a mom trying to do what she thought was best for her child had her bubble burst. "So I remember the summer hockey camp instructor on the middle of the ice saying, 'You should never play any other sport. Only hockey.'" It didn't make sense to Tabatha, but the instructor was well respected, so he should know, she reasoned. Tabatha followed the advice. Karsten was now focused only on hockey. "I think that's another reason why we become crazy. Because everyone around you is crazy. You've got these hockey camps that everyone goes into. And you've got the local coach saying, 'Let's do some spring hockey.' And if you don't do that, you don't fit in, so we better do that. Or we don't want him to be behind because everyone else is doing it. So we better do that. So we become crazy like everyone else."

And so Tabatha Leonard, like many good, caring hockey moms, was now all in on Karsten's hockey career. She still had no doubt at all; it was what Karsten wanted. "He had no other interests. Nothing. He didn't play with toys. He didn't play with anything. So we were like, 'Yeah, this is it.'"

Now there were hockey schools. And spring leagues. And plenty of travel. Gord and Tabatha both worked, but they were never rich. As hockey ramped up, somebody had to pay for it. "When my kids were growing up, we had no money, so both our parents paid for every hockey camp. And I wasn't afraid to ask for that. It was important to my kids. It was important to us that he did well. And that's where all our money went. I think that moms want whatever their kids want and will do anything that they need to do to get it."

In the early days of Karsten's minor hockey career, Tabatha saw the rink as an almost perfect environment. "At the beginning, you're all friends and, you know, aren't your kids cute? Let's get together and have drinks on weekends. Everyone is friends with everyone." She was at the rink all the time. Cheering. Supporting. Advocating. But as Karsten progressed, that happy place started to show its ugly side. "I guess it's competition. I guess people think that you think your kid is better than everybody else. I've had parents scream and yell at my kid on the ice to pass the puck or to stop scoring."

And god help the parent who attacks Tabatha's boy. "I made friends from hockey, but also, I think a lot of my hockey friends are no longer my friends because of hockey."

There were confrontations with parents from other teams. Sometimes, there were angry words exchanged with parents from her son's team. The confrontations never became physical, although there were times, she says, when it was touch and go. She was once removed from the stands at a game for yelling at a referee who was taking his time dropping a puck. "Like, I've been way worse before." There were times when Tabatha pounded so hard on the glass she would bend her wedding ring. While doing everything she could to help her kids make it as hockey players, she could not see that she was adding fuel to that awful stereotype of the crazy hockey mom. "Looking back, I think, 'Oh my god, why did I do that?'"

Both her boys were good players, but somehow her younger son, Heiden, managed to escape the drama. He was solid and had a knack for scoring in clutch situations, but he didn't dominate games the way Karsten often could. More importantly, he never made noises about wanting a career in hockey. His mother says, for Heiden, hockey was a pastime. Never anything more than that. "And I would say I was a different parent watching him play."

The drives to and from the rink were night and day for the two boys Tabatha says, maybe because expectations were so different. "With Heiden, it was like 'Have fun, buddy.' With Karsten, if he didn't play well, he heard about it on the way home from the rink and on the way to the rink. Like, it was two totally different things."

It took years for Tabatha to realize that Karsten and Heiden probably wanted the same from hockey. It took years for her to realize the pressure she was putting on Karsten without ever meaning to. "I always thought, to be honest, and it's embarrassing to say, but I did think that he was really good. And I thought he might have something."

The warning signs that Karsten's dreams had changed had been there for a long time, but Tabatha had missed them. Tabatha realized it when a Junior A scout came to watch Karsten. It was a perfect time to shine. Tabatha says Karsten knew the scout was there and played poorly. "We were like 'What the hell? You've got somebody watching you, and you barely did anything.'" Karsten answered honestly. He told his mom his poor play was by design. "He was like, 'I don't want to play there. I don't want them to look at me. I don't want that, and you guys are not listening to me. I don't want to move away from home. So I'll play like shit. So that way it doesn't happen.'"

That's when the light went on. That's when Tabatha Leonard realized that a young boy's dream of playing in the NHL had somehow become her dream. "So we had to really step back and say, 'What the hell are we doing?' I think we really had to check ourselves at the door."

From the day Karsten unloaded on his parents, Tabatha Leonard has been a different kind of hockey mom. She still hardly misses a game or a practice, but her expectations have evolved. "Is he a good hockey player? Yeah . . . He did not want to play hockey to make the OHL. He wanted to play hockey, have fun with his friends. And he always has. It's never been 'I want to play in the NHL.' That was our dream. That was never his dream. Do I wish he would have made it? I think his life may have been easier."

Tabatha Leonard lives with regrets. If she knew then what she knows now, she says, there are plenty of things she would have done differently. "I feel like we did him a disservice. I think we should have spent the same amount of time on school as we did on hockey. He barely passed many of his courses. Did we care? No. Hockey was more important."

Where she has no regrets at all is that very first decision to get her boys into a sport that is so much a part of small towns like hers. "I would still have put my kids in hockey. I would have done it a bit differently. But both my kids love hockey. It may not sound like they do. But both my kids love hockey."

Through all the ups and downs, including those difficult car drives, Tabatha believes hockey has been good for her boys, including Karsten. "He's street-smart, right? He can handle himself. I feel like when he has a job, he'll be able to handle his boss and know what to say and how to say it. Both my kids have had great championships and lots of fun and tournaments. My kids play ball hockey, and they've been able to go to Slovakia for Team Canada. And so there are things like that, where the experiences alone are phenomenal. And we would never give that back. There have been rough years, for sure. But my kids would still play hockey. I would never take that away from them."

Karsten now plays with his friends on a local Junior C team. It's not where his parents saw him landing, but it's the perfect fit for what he wants from hockey. In an unexpected twist, Heiden wound up on the same team. For the first time, Tabatha is able to watch her boys play together. And she no longer pounds on the glass or engages with the referees or other parents.

"Let your kid just have fun. Let your kid enjoy the game. Let them play with their friends. If my kid came to me today and said, 'Mom, I want to go to hockey camp this summer,' I'd be 'Great. Let's do it.' I would support them a thousand percent in hockey, no matter what. I would still be that crazy hockey mom. I'm just not going to scream and yell at you on the ice."

CHAPTER 6

Breaking the Ice Ceiling

"He couldn't even walk, and he was in the puck bucket being pulled around by my players on a bungee cord. He didn't even know that boys could play hockey. He was actually pretty excited to find out he can play. Because when he was at the rink, it was always my team playing, and all he saw were girls."
—Lisa Haley

LISA HALEY WAS AN assistant coach for the Canadian Olympic women's hockey team when they won gold in 2014. She has coached at the university level for nearly twenty-five years. She is now head coach of the women's hockey team at Ryerson University. She is also coaching the Hungarian women's national team. It's safe to say she knows how to coach. Yet around minor hockey rinks, especially on boys' teams, it's like her coaching career never happened. "I'm going to say, in general, my success as a coach in the female game carries very little weight."

Her son, Will, is a pretty good player. As he rose through the ranks of minor hockey, Lisa at one time thought she might have a thing or two to offer a bunch of talented young boys. She applied for a job with her son's team. She says the team turned her down. "Instead, it was a male who was never a head coach, even at the AAA level."

A few times, she volunteered to be an assistant coach. And more often than not, she ended up a passenger. Coaches with much less experience set up and ran the drills while the gold medal winner was never asked to do much more than play a support role. "I'm the puck pusher. Set up the pucks. Don't have any responsibility on the ice."

Women's hockey is among the fastest-growing sports in the world. Still, men continue to dominate the coaching ranks of both men's and women's hockey. In fact, most head coaches are men. It is rare to see a woman on the coaching staff of a men's team. Lisa Haley says coaching remains an old boys' club. "Every time you walk into a new environment as a female coach, you have to earn your stripes all over again. Whereas, if this was someone that had coached even a Tier 2 junior team as a guy and walked into this team, he would be respected as soon as he walked in the door. There's zero credit given to my resumé."

Lisa grew up in a hockey family in Nova Scotia. She played for her province in the 1991 Canada Winter Games, then had a solid career playing for Concordia University in Montreal. She moved back to her home province and worked as a physiotherapist at Saint Mary's University. When Saint Mary's began its first-ever women's hockey program in the late 1990s, Lisa was chosen to be its first head coach. "I really loved it from the beginning, and it really grew into a full-time career."

From there, it was on to coach women's hockey at Ryerson University in Toronto. In 2005, her only child, William, was born. It's no surprise, really, that he took to hockey. "He couldn't even walk, and he was in the puck bucket being pulled around by my players on a bungee cord. He didn't even know that boys could play hockey. He was actually pretty excited to find out he can play. Because when he was at the rink, it was always my team playing, and all he saw were girls."

Will began playing hockey when he was five and quickly moved into the competitive stream. Sitting in the stands with the other moms, watching their sons, convinced Lisa that she should put her skills to use and help the kids. "To generalize, most of the dads, they disregard me as a potential coach. It's the moms saying, 'Oh my god, why aren't you on the coaching staff?'"

It is a question, really, that many of the fathers should be asking.

As it was for Lisa Haley, hockey was always part of life for Jeanna Oke. Jeanna grew up in the small town of Marmora, Ontario, a few hours east of Toronto. She played boys' hockey first, until a girls' team was formed. "It's the best game in the world. I used to wait for my older cousins to get home from school so we could play hockey together. I think it's just the competitiveness of it and bringing people together the way it does."

Jeanna got married and had three boys—Ben, Jack, and Nick. When no other parent would step up to coach a novice team, her husband volunteered. And when he needed an assistant coach, Jeanna volunteered right away. Coaching was a natural fit: she had always been a strong athlete and had always loved hockey. "And that's the first time

I realized how much fun it was and the difference you could make in kids' lives."

As her sons evolved into competitive hockey players, Jeanna moved into the competitive coaching ranks. She was a woman filling a role that usually went to men, and there were plenty of hockey dads along the way who struggled with it. "There's been some tough moments with some of those men for sure," she says. But parents like to see their kids be part of winning teams, and Jeanna Oke knows how to win. "Without sounding too conceited, there haven't been too many times I've coached a team where we haven't finished first or won a championship or won most of the tournaments that we've been in."

She sticks with it even though her sons are done with minor hockey. She knows she has something to offer. And deep down, despite the odd negative comment, she loves it. "I'm at the rink a lot, but I wouldn't change it for anything. And I think I'm proud of what I can offer now, and how I've grown my game and how I've helped different players."

As she rose through the coaching ranks, Jeanna sought guidance from others who were doing similar jobs. Their advice, she says, followed a template that has been part of minor hockey for years. "A lot of that came from the people who were mentoring me at the time, who were great hockey people and important men in hockey. And it was like, you don't have to talk to the parents, and don't worry about the parents. Looking back on that, I think that was the wrong approach. That's one of the things you learn along the way."

Initially, as a woman trying hard to fit into a world dominated by men, she followed the counsel she was given and remained a bit distant with parents. Often she was hard on her players. It was her youngest son, Nick, whom she coached through AAA, who helped soften her approach. He wanted to be a coach and went looking to his mom for advice. She thought a bit and told him, "I like to win, first and foremost. Still, no matter what happens, every time a player leaves the rink, they should feel good about themselves." Even after a player's worst game, she told her son, they should not feel like the sky is falling down. "Tell them this is what we're going to work on next. They need to leave the rink feeling good about themselves every single time."

Her son absorbed the advice. And he told his mom, who had been his coach for so many years, "There's a lot of times I left the rink and didn't feel that way."

That simple, honest comment from her son made Jeanna reflect on who she was as a coach. She realized there were many things she could have done differently, both as a hockey mom and as a hockey coach. "Starting out as a coach, you're super competitive. You want to win, and it's probably a little bit more about yourself at the time, because you're trying to build your resumé and prove yourself. But now my game has grown so much as a coach, and some of that is because of the negatives and a lot of it's because of the positives."

Jeanna has taken all the advice she's been given, the good and the bad, and modified it to develop her own style. Through her years of experience, she has evolved into a different kind of coach. "I've really made the transition and now talk to the parents. It's important to have them as your friends, and I think that's where a lot of the support comes from."

Parents now line up to have their kids be part of her skills development programs and spring hockey teams. And she gets plenty of calls from young coaches starting out and looking for advice. "There were times when people would sort of look down on me because I'm a woman and coaching, but I think that my resumé and my success sort of speaks for itself now."

LISA HALEY CONTINUES TO build an impressive resumé in women's hockey. She has been part of high-performance camps for some of the top women players in the world. But she has faced some challenges as she's settled into the role of hockey mom with her son, Will.

Will started out in the highly competitive Greater Toronto Hockey League. He was good enough to make top teams, but never good enough to star on those teams. Always, Lisa sensed an unhealthy pressure being put on the players and the coaches, and it was coming from the parents. "Coaches are worried about how many wins they have, and parents are worried about the number of centres on a team. 'If my son plays on this team, then I want only two. I want him to play every second shift.' It just seems to have really evolved on an unethical pathway."

A couple of years before the 2014 Olympics, Lisa and her family moved to Calgary, the home base for Canada's women's hockey team. It meant uprooting Will and getting him into a minor hockey program in Calgary. Then a coach from Toronto called with advice. He suggested that Will return to Toronto so he would stay on the radar of scouts and coaches. Will was seven years old. Lisa and her husband followed the advice. "And I remember my husband and my son choosing to pack everything up and moving back to Toronto so that he could finish the season with his North York hockey team."

Sure enough, back in Toronto, her son made a top AAA team. "And we think, 'Wow. Thank god we did that.' Then you think, how crazy are we and everyone else that we're choosing where we're living in Canada so that our son, as a seven-year-old, can get into the AAA loop."

It was a learning experience. After three years of Will trying out for teams in the GTHL, Lisa and her husband said enough. "We actually decided this is a disgusting experience for us." They moved about an hour east of Toronto. Away from big-city pressures, Lisa says the fit has been perfect. "Will has got an unbelievably fantastic coaching staff that we love, and he's knocking it out of the park. Whether that's the mom speaking or the professional coach speaking, I guess it's a bit of both. But it's been a really great environment for him."

LISA HALEY BELIEVES HOCKEY would be a better game if more women were involved in coaching, especially in women's hockey. "It is still not the norm to have females coaching in the female game in minor hockey. I just think that females need female role models. There's a lot of great male coaches out there, and I know many of them. I'm proud to say that they're a part of our game. At the same time, there are many youth coaches that are trying to coach like you're in the NHL. At youth hockey, it shouldn't matter who wins."

Priorities need to shift, she believes. She is hoping the focus in hockey returns to developing skills and good people. "Youth hockey coaches are coaching the way professional coaches coach. And they think they're doing it right. And they're doing it completely wrong. It's got to be about development. The individual players should be given every opportunity to reach their full potential. That's our responsibility."

These are lessons that some coaches will never learn. Jeanna Oke learned them through trial and error. When she started out, she was hard on her players, emulating what she had seen in other coaches. The longer she survived, the more she allowed herself to show a softer side that maybe comes with being a mother. "I think, as a mom, you just have that little bit of compassion—for young players, especially. And I'm not saying that men don't do the same thinking, but I think there was a little bit more awareness of maybe just their feelings."

Jeanna has developed into one of Ontario's top minor hockey coaches. In 2022, her two teams each won Ontario Minor Hockey Association Championships, and she is sought after for her ability to develop young players. After coaching high-level boys' hockey for well over a decade now, Jeanna has some advice for coaches just starting out: "I think most young coaches take it personally if you lose, and you take it personally if you win, and it becomes a little bit about yourself. And that's the number one thing I would say to young coaches is that it isn't about you at all. It's about the players, and right now, for me, it's all about the players."

Lisa Haley would love to see hockey reconnect to its roots, to a time when the game was simpler and maybe less of the business it has become. "When we were kids, I played hockey because I wanted to, not because my parents wanted me to. That's definitely changed. And we had to figure out a way to get to games and practices and tournaments. Nowadays, their parents make sure they get to the rink on time and organize their drives and their snacks and the post-game shakes and everything else. Everything is just perfect for the kids to thrive. That's not real. That's not what real life is all about."

The hockey world isn't perfect. But Lisa is convinced it can be a much better sport simply by opening more doors to women like her who change lives through coaching. "So many minor hockey coaches, which are typically men, are so caught up in the X's and O's. There is little focus on relationship building, confidence building, and teaching skills and concepts. I think in general, just personality-wise, females do want that."

Her hope: maybe, just maybe, more women will be given that opportunity.

CHAPTER 7

Motorcycle Marj: The Mother of All Hockey Mothers

"When I think back now, I think, 'How many people get to do that?'
Not too many. It was pretty phenomenal to play with
your mom, when you look back at it."
—Theresa Morrison

MARJ MORRISON GREW UP on a farm in southern Manitoba that was first settled by her grandparents well over a century ago. The southern reaches of her land touched North Dakota along the US border. They had a bit of everything on the farm—cows, pigs, horses, chickens, and grains. She and her brother, Gordon, did their part to keep the farm going.

When Marj was thirteen, in the late 1940s, a hockey coach started up the first girls' team in the area, and Marj was one of the first recruits. She loved sports and was a natural athlete. She was a skilled figure skater and figured, why not hockey? They played their games in an indoor rink, but with natural ice. The pigeons liked hanging out in the rink; it was a good place to stay warm. The pigeon poop all over the ice somehow just seemed to add to the atmosphere.

Marj played for a few years and liked hockey well enough. But boys and the rest of life got in the way. Marj tucked away her hockey experiences, not realizing how important the game would become to her later in life.

Marj was sixteen when she went to her mom and asked for a car. Her mom said no but offered to buy Marj a motorcycle instead. Soon enough, she was riding around the farm roads of southern Manitoba on a 1953 BSA, a motorcycle built by a British company that went under twenty years later. The motorcycle became her freedom. When there were dances in Goodlands and other nearby towns, she'd hop on her bike, with a friend on the back, and off they'd go. Marj kept and rode the bike all her life. It has been completely restored by her son. Her nickname, "Motorcycle Marj," fit so perfectly.

Marj remained on the family farm. She got married and had six kids in ten years, five of them girls. The youngest was a year old when Marj's husband left them. He just walked away and never came back. All those kids, the farm, and only Marj to do it all. As you can imagine, life wasn't easy.

It was around this time that hockey made a triumphant return to Marj's life. The women's hockey team from Marj's youth hadn't survived very long. But by the time she had all those kids, another coach had come along to start a new women's league in the early 1970s. Marj with all her girls—you almost had a team right there. And if her girls were going to play, Marj was going to play too. A single mom with five girls, playing hockey together.

Marj began her comeback playing centre. "I was fairly fast. I could skate pretty good." When age started catching up, she dropped back to defence. When age really caught up, she became a goaltender. "I was pretty good. Wasn't afraid of it. Like some people were afraid of it. But I wasn't."

Plenty of women in southern Manitoba signed up to play hockey. Eventually, there were seven teams. Year after year, nobody could touch the team featuring the Morrison girls, Marj and her gang.

Theresa, the second-youngest daughter, says early on, it was old-style hockey. Raw and physical. A bad day on the farm? No worries. Take out those aggressions on the ice. "The only equipment they ever wore was a helmet and skates. Most of them didn't even have hockey gloves. Some of them would maybe have shin pads. Full body contact. Slapshots." They played in figure skates at first. But it all got "high-end" pretty fast: hockey skates, full equipment. The women of southern Manitoba were getting serious. "It was a big change for us for hockey," Theresa says.

The Morrison girls could all skate and play with skill. And they were tough as nails. Theresa says good luck to the player who took liberties with their mother, Marj. "Then you'd have to get them for getting your mother."

Theresa remembers the time all of the girls in her family, including Marj, were recruited to help fill out a ringette tournament. "It didn't go well," she says matter-of-factly. The Morrison girls ended up being tossed from the tournament. "I guess we were too aggressive. Lean on your stick, and nobody is taking the ring. That's what we did. Then we just lifted everybody's stick and took the ring, and we'd go in and score. They were like, 'Well, this isn't right.' Can't help it. It's a stupid sport. Hockey is great."

Another time, the Morrison girls made history by playing in an exhibition game in 1975 against an all-star team from Brandon, Manitoba. The game was a big deal, and a local radio station carried it live. It was the first time a women's game was broadcast live. The Morrison girls won big. Marj even threw a sweater on her ten-year-old daughter Brenda so she could step on the ice and be part of the historic game.

The Morrisons were good overall athletes, just like their mom. Theresa remembers competing in high school track meets, and her mom pulling up on her motorcycle to watch. Sports became a break from reality during a difficult time for a young family. And in many ways, Theresa says, hockey was the family's glue. "When I think back now, I think, 'How many people get to do that?' Not too many. It was pretty phenomenal to play with your mom, when you look back at it."

Their life was good, but it was far from easy. Marj had to sell off chunks of the farm to bring in some cash. "Sometimes, we didn't even have enough money to buy a pencil, but we got through it." They all pitched in, just as their mother had a generation earlier. With food from the farm, Marj made sure her family never went hungry. She was a fabulous cook. She had shelves stacked with preserves. "It wasn't all fun and games, and I mean, there were things that were hard to do," Theresa says. "I definitely couldn't have done what she did."

The only boy in the family, Bob, ended up working in the oil field.

Most of the sisters stayed close to home, but Brenda, the middle sister, moved to a small Quebec community about an hour north of Ottawa. She had two sons and, just like her mother, became a single mom when her kids were young. Just like her mom, her go-to became hockey. Brenda joined a women's league in the area, and the skills she had developed on the ice in southern Manitoba all came flooding back. Her skating, shooting, and passing made her a star in her league.

When Brenda's two boys were old enough, they played hockey too. Both Derrick and Dusty seemed to love the game just as much as she did. There was no doubt in her mind that she would raise her children the same way she was raised. She was a single mom, and she structured life around hockey. If there was homework, it had to be finished before hockey. That had been Marj's rule when Brenda was a kid, and it became her rule too. One time her younger son, Dusty, showed up at the rink without his homework done. His team had a game that night, and Brenda's rule was firm. "I brought the homework with me. And he had to sit in the front entrance and do his homework on a table before he could go on the ice. The coach was coming to me and saying, 'Hey, we need Dusty on the ice. He's our number one goalie.' Well, he never did make it on the ice. I never had to worry about that happening again."

Brenda was one of those moms who coached her boys, beginning with Derrick when he was five. She couldn't leave Dusty alone in the arena, so Brenda dressed him in hockey gear and brought him on the ice, hoping he would hang around quietly. Good luck. "And he would be mad at me because I wasn't paying much attention to him. He would lie against the boards with a water bottle. Then he would have to pee. Finally, I said, 'Just go in the net there. You can play there. And sometimes the puck will come your way, and just put your stick on the ice and push it away.' Next thing you know, he's hanging in the net upside down."

That was the start of Dusty's goaltending career. He loved stopping pucks and remained a goaltender all through hockey. "He was the kid that was always happy. He loved the challenge. Like shootouts; he lived for that. And I'm always so stressed about that. It's just the way he is."

As Brenda navigated her world as a single mom, she closely followed the path blazed by her mother. She says Marj raised her kids in a house filled with plenty of love and common sense. "Strong woman. Very strong. She was the mother and the father. She taught us to think for ourselves and have good judgment. And I think that's how it is with hockey. Hockey teaches you how to win and lose. And that's kind of what life's about."

As Brenda got older, she realized more and more how important hockey had become in her life. It's what she knew. "I was the hockey player. And I was the coach. And I was the hockey mom." It was not always easy. "We had a group of friends, and we would all help one another. Even with hockey equipment, you know, passing skates to other kids."

Brenda's kids took to hockey the same way she had. Derrick was a smart hockey player who could play any position with skill. Just like his mom, he could skate like the wind. Dusty was always in demand because he was good at stopping pucks. Her boys' greatest thrill, Brenda says, was those times when they played together. "Derrick was always defending his little brother in the net. They were inseparable on the ice and in all aspects of their lives. Just like my mother taught us, family is number one. Hockey is the foundation that built their bond."

Hockey was Brenda's sport, and she was pleased to see it had become their sport too. Still, she often worried that her kids might feel they had no say in the matter. As they got older, she made sure they knew they were free to quit anytime they wanted; hockey didn't always have to be part of their lives. "If they don't like the challenge. Or they don't like the competition or organized sports, then that's not the area for them. Go in a different direction, in the arts or something like that."

Neither boy ever did drift away from hockey. They kept playing even as they became involved in professional motocross. "The physical and mental skills they developed playing hockey helped them find success on the motocross track." Both of her sons are now certified welders and crane operators, and they both still play hockey. So does Brenda, who is closing in on sixty.

Having raised two boys as a single mom, Brenda wonders now how her mother, Marj, managed to make it work on her own with six kids. "Life was stressful for her. It was tough. I don't remember how tough it was. It all seemed normal to me."

Marj was well into her fifties before she finally gave up playing hockey. By then, her son had moved away from home. Her girls were young women and starting lives of their own. Marj always believed hockey was the touchstone that kept the family unit strong. "All of us doing something together. Stayed together that way." She had many grandchildren and great-grandchildren who played hockey. Marj was always a regular at their games.

The game gave them so many good memories. But nothing lasts forever. The farm that was part of the family for generations has been sold. In 2019, the oldest Morrison girl, Donna, died suddenly of heart failure. And in 2021, Marj passed away. It was a good life but a difficult one. Her body simply wore out. She was a few months short of her eighty-fifth birthday.

The girls learned so much from their mother through the game of hockey. Theresa, who still lives near the old family farm, is a teacher. What she was taught as a kid, she now teaches her students. "You want something, you have to work for it. So when they are having trouble with a concept, I relate it to hockey. 'How many times did you practise the slapshot before you got it right?' You can always make that correlation back to hockey."

Theresa says Marj—a tough and wise single mom who got it right—took a difficult situation and found a way to build something special. "I definitely couldn't have done what she did. Strength and work ethic. That's what she taught us. And leave things the way you found them or better."

The lasting legacy of Motorcycle Marj, who left the world a much better place.

CHAPTER 8

Blazing a Brand-New Trail

"I woke up with butterflies in my stomach. I called my mom. I said, 'Is this normal?' My mom said, 'It's payback time.' At that moment, we had an understanding: My god, did I put her through this?"
—Manon Rhéaume

THE MOTHER OF ONE of women's hockey's greatest icons never imagined her daughter would be remembered as a trailblazer, for blowing doors open for women hockey players everywhere. Nicole Rhéaume remembers her daughter, Manon, as a little girl who just wanted to play hockey. "I saw her so much playing hockey with her brothers. They were shooting pucks at her. She had all the gear on."

From an early age, Manon loved the challenge of trying to stop pucks. And right from the beginning, she was good. "My brothers pretty much used me as a target," she says. "And anytime I wanted to do girly things, they'd be like, 'Oh, come play with us.'"

Manon Rhéaume was born in 1972 in the ski community of Lac-Beauport, about half an hour north of Quebec City. Her father, Pierre, built an outdoor rink for all of the kids in the community to use. He also coached hockey. Often he struggled to find a goaltender. Manon remembers, "We were at the dinner table, and he would say, 'We're going to a tournament and nobody is showing interest to play goalie.' And I'd say, 'Why not me? I'm doing it with my brothers all the time.' That's how I got started."

It was a time and a community, like many others, where girls just didn't play. "I was pretty much the only one. It took years before I saw other girls." If she was going to play hockey, it would have to be with boys. And it would be with her father coaching. "It's true that I didn't want her to play hockey," Nicole says. "Luckily, Pierre was always there to take care of it because he was the coach."

A little girl who wanted to play hockey. That's how a historic hockey journey began. "At a young age, there was no pressure at first. Because I was just playing the game, and I loved it. And it was fun."

THERE WERE PLENTY OF parents grumbling about a girl taking up a spot on a boys' team. They were just whispers at first, but they got louder, and they eventually found their way to Manon's dad. Another father would approach Pierre and offer his son as a replacement for Manon. The kid was pretty good at stopping balls while playing street hockey, the father would say. Pierre would always give the kid a shot. He knew that facing tennis balls outside was not the same as stopping pucks. And he knew that his daughter was good. "My dad would say, 'Trust me,'" Manon says. "And sure enough, the kid would go in, play goalie. We would lose thirteen to three. All of the parents would go back to my dad after and say, 'We want her back in net.'"

While this was going on, Nicole watched nervously. When other parents complained about having a girl on the team, she kept quiet. "I could hear the comments. And it was hurtful. I didn't want to create problems. And I never shared those things with Manon. I didn't want it to bother her or hurt her or worry her."

Manon didn't need to be told. She heard it too. Sometimes not so subtly, like the time she made a couple of impressive saves off a player from another team. In the handshake line after the game, the player who couldn't score on Manon punched her in the gut. Just like her mom, she said and did nothing. "For me, I wouldn't tell my parents because I didn't want to be a tattletale. I didn't want to be that person."

Decades later, Manon is only now realizing that she and her mother shared the same strategy: don't make waves. "It's funny that she wouldn't share with me the things that people were saying, to protect me. And I wasn't sharing stuff that I had to deal with, so I would be accepted. So we were both keeping stuff to ourselves."

The only girl playing boys' minor hockey in Lac Beauport in the late 1970s was tiny and determined. Where would it lead? Her mother had no idea. "When Manon was younger," Nicole says, "I was beginning to realize she was the first girl doing a lot of things in hockey."

Her father had no problem allowing Manon to play on his teams, but there were plenty of other coaches along the way who said no.

Before tryouts, they would tell Pierre, "Don't bring your daughter. We're not taking a girl on the team." But he still brought her, without telling her she had no chance. She would try out, she would get cut, and she would be disappointed. But Pierre saw that getting cut made her work harder and want it more. "For me," Manon says, "I was just playing hockey. And I was trying every year to make it to the highest level."

Manon's mother watched it all unfold, and still she remained silent. "One of the most ridiculous things I heard was that Manon was taking the spot of their kid, who was going to make it to the NHL someday. Sometimes other parents would avoid me just because they didn't like the fact that Manon was a girl."

Plenty of other parents offered encouragement. They saw Manon's talent and determination, and they wanted her to succeed. At the same time, as she got older, the pressure grew. "The spotlight was on her," Nicole says. "The pressure she was living, to be perfect as a girl. I was living it too, as a mother."

By the time Manon reached peewee, almost everyone in hockey in Lac-Beauport knew who she was. In 1984, she became the first girl to play in the famous Québec International Pee-Wee Hockey Tournament. It was her coming-out party. She played well, and suddenly people outside of her hometown were buzzing about the tiny girl who was just as good or even better than the boys.

Manon remembers being invited to a photo shoot at a Quebec Nordiques practice—an eleven-year-old girl on the same ice as an NHL team. "And one reporter wrote, 'Maybe one day Manon could make it to the NHL.' At eleven. And it went right over my head," she laughs. "I was thinking, 'No woman can ever play in the NHL. Never going to happen.'"

She was eighteen years old when she finally played on her first girls' team. It was in Sherbrooke, Quebec, nearly two and a half hours from home. A year later she became the first female goalie to play in the Quebec Major Junior Hockey League. She was the third goaltender for the Trois-Rivières Draveurs, and she played on the same team as her younger brother, Pascal. In many ways, it became an audition for what was to follow.

THE TAMPA BAY LIGHTNING joined the NHL in 1992. A new team tasked with drawing fans in a non-traditional hockey market made plenty of noise by inviting Manon to be part of their first training camp. She had just led Canada to a gold medal at the Women's World Championship. Now she was competing with eight other goaltenders trying to win a job in the NHL. Her critics had a field day.

"My story," Manon says, "and how it's told now, compared to then, it's totally different." Not surprisingly, the narrative then was not flattering. One newspaper drew comparisons between her tryout and the days of circus freak shows. "I kind of blocked it out and continued doing what I was doing," she says.

The attention was non-stop. There was a feature on her in *People* magazine. She had a guest appearance on the *Late Show with David Letterman*. "I had no clue who he was," she says. "It was not until later, years later, living in the US and seeing who was on his show, it was like, 'Oh my god, I can't believe I was on his show.' I realized then it was a big deal."

She was twenty years old, and people were debating whether or not she belonged. All Manon wanted was a chance to prove she belonged. She got to training camp and put on a show. Most of the other eight goaltenders invited to camp were long gone by the time she got her chance to start a pre-season game. She played a period in a game against St. Louis, gave up two goals on nine shots, and walked away with her head held high. "It was a 2–2 game when I left the game. Nobody could say, 'Oh, it was awful. She was terrible. She didn't belong there.' And to me, that was my biggest pride of the camp."

Manon's mom and dad were back home, watching on television as their daughter made history. "I was always nervous for every game," her mother remembers. "But for that game Manon played in Tampa, my husband and I took little pills to calm our nerves. We couldn't handle how fast our hearts were beating."

Three decades later, Manon laughs at her mom's words. "I didn't know that."

It was another one of those moments when Nicole Rhéaume watched her daughter achieve a first for women in hockey without necessarily seeing the bigger picture. "A lot of people have told me over the years that she was a pioneer. What she did really helped open doors to other girls. Obviously, when I hear that from other people, I feel extra pride for what she has done."

After the Tampa experience, Manon had further hockey adventures.

She played in another exhibition game the following season, against Boston. She played a few games on minor league teams and became the first woman ever to play in a professional game during the regular season. "Every time someone would say no to me or doubt me, you wanted to prove people wrong. That was part of my motivation. I wanted to keep going higher."

There was international success too, in women's hockey. She was an all-world all-star twice, helping Canada win gold at the Women's World Championship. And in 1998, she played three games for Canada at the Olympics in Nagano, Japan, with her mom and dad there watching. She came home with a silver medal. Nicole says, "That was a special moment." Being in Nagano for Manon is one of her favourite memories from her days as a hockey mom.

MANON'S YOUNGER BROTHER, PASCAL, is also a pretty good story. They are sixteen months apart. Pascal was never one of those kids who everybody said was going to make it. But he did.

Pascal loved hockey and worked hard to improve his game. He was never drafted by an NHL team, but he ended up with a tryout with the New Jersey Devils and eventually made the team. He had a seventeen-year professional career that included a Stanley Cup championship and an American Hockey League championship.

Nicole realizes her son was never a star, and that may be her biggest source of pride when it comes to his career. "A lot of people didn't think he would ever make it. He worked hard. He was a smart player. He was a playmaker. Someone gave him a chance. He had a chance to make it. So I'm really proud."

Nicole and Pierre would drive hours to watch Pascal play in junior or in nearby NHL rinks. He played more than three hundred NHL games. For a hockey-loving mother, having a son in the NHL was exciting. "It was not as nerve-wracking watching Pascal play, because he was a forward, not a goalie. It's easier to be the parent of a forward. Every time he was on TV, we wouldn't miss a game."

STUDIES HAVE SUGGESTED THAT reading to a child in the womb helps develop language skills. Manon Rhéaume wonders if something similar happened for her boys, who both became hockey players. "My kids, they heard pucks flying all over the place while they were still in me."

Her elder son, Dylan, was born in 1999. He started as a forward, moved to defence, and eventually followed his mother's lead and became a goaltender. "And now I can relate to my mom," Manon says with a smile. "When I watch, it's not fun. Dylan had this big game, and I woke up with butterflies in my stomach. I called my mom. I said, 'Is this normal?' My mom said, 'It's payback time.' At that moment, we had an understanding: My god, did I put her through this?"

Dylan has risen through the ranks of the American hockey program (Manon has lived in the United States all her adult life). When Dylan was eighteen years old, he joined the University of Notre Dame's hockey program. He spent four years there before transferring to Quinnipiac University in Connecticut in 2021. Just like his mom, Dylan is technically sound, mentally tough, and quick. And just like his mom, he faces huge obstacles as he tries to carve out a path in professional hockey. For Manon, it was a gender issue. For Dylan, it's his size. He is five-foot-eight at a time when goaltenders are giants. "My older son has been pushed to overcome and prove people wrong. Now in professional hockey, they are looking for six feet and up," his mother says. "He has to deal with a lot of stuff I had to deal with. He may still get a shot. You never know. But I'm so proud of how he has handled adversity along the way."

Some parents love it when a child follows in their footsteps. Not Manon Rhéaume. "At first, I was kind of like, 'Cool. That's my position.' I soon discovered that I wish he didn't play goalie, because it's the worst thing to be the mom of a goalie."

It has not been all bad, and Manon sees that. "Along the way, we had this kind of bond. We could understand each other when it comes to hockey. It's a cool bond that I know I'll be able to share with him for the rest of our lives." They talk about goals Dylan let in. Or saves he made. But more as goalie to goalie. "I get it. I get how he feels in a certain situation."

In 2006, along came a second son, Dakoda. "And I was like, please don't pick goalie. I cannot do two goalies."

Dakoda chose to play defence. And he's good at it. He has been groomed in the elite hockey programs of Detroit, where his mom now lives. "I always say I enjoy going to see both of my kids play. But when I watch my older one, it's not fun. My stomach is so nervous. And when I'm watching my younger one, I'm enjoying the game even more."

Manon's mom and dad still live in Quebec, just north of the St. Lawrence River. Manon doesn't see her mother much, but they talk just about every day, she says. "It's amazing to see they're still supporting everything that I do as an adult. I had great parents that taught me how to be there for your kids. They taught me so much. And that's how I want to be with my kids."

The family got together in the late summer of 2021. Manon was back home to be honoured for all she has done to create more opportunities for women in hockey. Her parents were with her in Quebec City as a life-size bronze statue of a young Manon Rhéaume was unveiled.

When she and her mom were together, they went through boxes and boxes of memories. Nicole kept every clipping, every puck, every program with Manon's name on it. Manon was blown away by her mom's collection of souvenirs. Their bond remains as strong as ever. "We are very much alike," Nicole says. "How she is with her boys is much like how it was with us when she played."

Twenty years after her pre-season game with Tampa, she caught up with Terry Crisp, her former head coach with the Lightning. She knew he hadn't been a fan of having a woman on his team. With the benefit of time and reflection, Crisp told her that she was good at training camp and got the opportunity to play in that exhibition game because she earned it. "I didn't care that it took me twenty years to hear that," she says. "It felt really, really good."

She understands that she was able to make a name for herself because there were people who believed in her. It started with her dad and mom, and continued with everyone who opened a door and gave her a chance. "Some people really saw something in me. It took years to see that, because the negative things sometimes take over or give you doubt of why you were there. It feels good to realize that, even if it has taken forty-nine years to get there."

The game of hockey has been good for Manon Rhéaume, and she has helped it become the sport of choice for hundreds of thousands of girls and women around the world. At the 2022 NHL All-Star Skills Competition, she inspired still more young hockey players as one of the goalies in net for the Breakaway Challenge.

A large part of Manon's success was thanks to Nicole, who allowed her daughter to dream big and go for it. Now, Manon finds pure joy in watching her two sons play. It doesn't really matter whether they make it to the highest level, she says. "They are good people and part of a game that can transform lives. They're going to learn so many amazing lessons that will help them later in life."

CHAPTER 9

Pride and Dreams

"If anybody has an opportunity to be a role model to the next generation,
that's an obligation we have. It's great for Indigenous kids to see that through
hard work you can achieve some of your goals and dreams in life."
—Donna Young McCormick

YOU NEVER KNOW WHAT the future holds when a kid steps on the ice
for the first time. For future NHL player Cody McCormick, his first
time on skates was not pleasant. "Apparently, I forgot to take the skate
guards off," his mother says. Donna Young McCormick was about to
be a hockey mom but had no background in the game. She had no
clue, really, where to even begin. "I got to the local rink. I had absolutely no idea how to put all of the equipment on my two kids."

Other parents stepped in to help Donna navigate those early days,
and Cody and his older brother, Jesse, comfortably settled into a
hockey routine. Donna says Cody, especially, loved the game almost

immediately. "I can remember him sitting there at the age of five, telling me he wanted to play in the NHL. At that age, you're thinking, 'Okay, and so does every other kid.'"

But both her boys were growing into good hockey players. And Donna, the hockey novice, was quickly coming to understand that the game could become all-consuming. They lived in Mount Brydges, a rural community in southern Ontario, and every game—every practice, it seemed—was a road trip, Jesse heading to one rink, Cody to another. "Our life revolved around that hockey calendar on the fridge."

Donna says hockey was a family project. She and her husband, Chris, shared the load in making hockey work for their two boys. Their schedule took them to many Little Native Hockey League ("Little NHL") tournaments during spring breaks, even as far as Finland and the Czech Republic, where Cody played with Indigenous players from across Canada.

Both Donna and Chris had good jobs. Donna worked as an education consultant with the First Nations. Chris was a respected leader in the community and was elected Grand Chief of the Association of Iroquois and Allied Indians. They always had family around to help ferry the kids to their games and practices. And still, Donna says, making it all work was a struggle. "Tournaments may be in two different cities, and paying for hotels and dinners with teammates and families, it meant during the hockey season you were very much a part of the hockey family."

Donna could see Jesse developing interests outside of hockey. But Cody never really did. The idea of playing in the NHL that he hatched when he was five years old never left him. "Over the years, I saw his drive and commitment and passion for the game. And you start thinking, maybe he will stick with this."

When Cody was ten years old, a AAA team was launched in his community. He made the team. Donna says that's when his game really took off. "If you're talking about a Wayne Gretzky, scoring all the goals, no, he wasn't that guy. But he was the guy providing leadership. He would be the liaison to the coach. And he would provide toughness and grit, that determination for the game that inspired other players. I would say that's what got him to the professional level."

Donna marvelled at Cody's determination to get to where he wanted to be in hockey, even after a teacher told his class that none of them would play in the NHL and they should stop dreaming about it. "There were many sacrifices he made. He missed school events and different parties for practices and tournaments and travel with his team because his focus was on hockey. I think he was one of those players from a very young age who just knew what he wanted to do. I sat down with him at fourteen and said, 'If you're still interested in a career in hockey, what are we going to do now? What is the plan going to be?' And we talked about things like power skating and hockey camps. He was very focused. It was his journey. Chris and I just tried to support him as much as possible."

In so many ways, Cody was a perfect power forward. He was big and skilled. And Donna says by the time he was ready for junior hockey, scouts had taken notice. "He could score the points. He could set up goals. He could hand out great bodychecks. After a while you would be seeing the same scouts at different tournaments and games. And they would start talking to us. In our case, it was the Belleville Bulls."

Cody was sixteen when his name was called at an OHL draft. He was a second-round pick of the Belleville Bulls. And he made the team that first year. "You can imagine, we were a little surprised he would be leaving home and living in a small town like Belleville. We are a tight-knit family, and we missed having him, but we thought it was a great opportunity, and he wanted to go."

His mother says the Belleville experience was gold. He landed with a caring billet family, the Sylvesters, and remained with them for all four of his seasons in Belleville. "You have faith that this family is going to look after your child and provide for him and feed him and make sure he gets to games. And they get next to nothing for it. We had a great billet family. They were amazing."

Cody was a wonderful mix of size, toughness, and skill. His leadership skills and maturity were evident early in his career. He was named team captain his final junior season by a unanimous vote of the players and became one of his team's top scorers. For Donna, that season remains among her favourite hockey memories. "He took on that leadership role, and it was very exciting for him. He had a breakout year in scoring. He was also a good bodychecker and got awards for being an unsung hero."

After his first two seasons with the Bulls, Cody and his entire family went to the 2001 NHL draft in Florida. Donna had absolutely no expectations of where or when he would be selected. They just wanted to be there for him when his name was called. It happened in the fifth round. He was taken by the Colorado Avalanche. "It gets a little tense. You hope you go in the second day, but it might not happen. Then his name gets called. You get the jersey. And then things happen pretty quickly. The team sweeps in. You're having photos taken and doing interviews. It's a new world."

As they watched Cody play his final two seasons in Belleville, the Colorado Avalanche began to understand that they might have stumbled on a gem in the 2001 draft. The year after his breakout junior season, Cody was playing in the NHL. After so many years of work and sacrifice, he had made it. "His father and I would go down to training camp," Donna remembers. "The first season he was selected to stay with the team was exciting. He was playing with players like Peter Forsberg and Joe Sakic and Rob Blake, Teemu Selänne and Adam Foote. To watch that first game, in an NHL rink, and watch your son take his first shift was very exciting."

For a mother whose son had dreamed all his life about being an NHL player, the time just sort of flew by once he got there. Cody McCormick played thirteen seasons of professional hockey and racked up more than four hundred NHL games playing with the Colorado Avalanche, Minnesota Wild, and Buffalo Sabres. It was all so satisfying for Donna, watching as Cody realized his dream. "A lot of players, even first-rounders, might not even play one NHL game. He managed to beat the odds. Yes, we are very proud of him."

What ended Cody's hockey career was an unexpected health issue, a blood clot in his lung that resulted from an injury. He was almost thirty-two when he played his final NHL game. "It was quite scary," Donna says. "You're looking at some bigger issues besides your career and the game. You're looking at the quality of life."

Donna Young McCormick is proud of how hard her son worked to make it in hockey. She is equally pleased that he never shied away from who he is or where he is from. Cody was close with his grandfather, who was a residential school survivor. "We are very proud of our cultural identity. Cody is of Chippewa and Oneida heritage, and he's a member of the Chippewas of the Thames First Nation. If anybody has an opportunity to be a role model to the next generation, that's an obligation we have. It's great for Indigenous kids to see that through hard work you can achieve some of your goals and dreams in life."

Since he retired from hockey, Cody has travelled extensively to First Nations communities across North America. He does speaking engagements and runs hockey clinics. His mother says he is living proof that it's okay to dream big. "If they can see a role model who looks like them and is from their same background, I think it can go a long way in helping them focus their lives and find a healthy path to what they want to achieve."

Cody's brother, Jesse, turned his focus to academics once his minor hockey career ran its course. He became a lawyer after earning law degrees at both the University of Ottawa and Harvard University. He has spent his adult life working on Indigenous issues, including environmental protection and economic development. Twice he ran for a seat in the House of Commons. "He's had an impressive career too," his mother says. "And all the time he spent in hockey rinks certainly helped him. You become a team player. You win and you lose as a group together. Maybe there is a bit of compromise, a bit of negotiation in there as well."

Although Donna never expected to be a hockey mom, it became a big part of her life. "It's been a wonderful journey. It goes very quickly. It can go by in the blink of an eye, so enjoy it."

She and Chris worked together to help their two sons follow two very different career paths—one in the NHL, the other as a Harvard-educated lawyer—and each has excelled. Donna says, "Stay tuned. There's lots more to see from both our boys."

CHAPTER 10

Knowing When to Push

"It's hard to know when to push them and when not to. But I think when it's fear in the way, you kind of have to prepare them that anything can happen. You're never going to know until you try."
—Katie Wakely

IT WOULD BE HARD to know it by watching her at the rink, but Katie Wakely sometimes struggles with hockey. Not the game itself, but all the noise from the game. Angry and petty parents? She has no time for any of that. She is not that mother banging on the glass or leading cheers. In fact, she often sits alongside the timekeeper, away from the fans, at her sons' games, pumping out music from the scorekeeper's area. If she's not there, she is probably sitting with family, away from the hockey moms. It is her way of escaping the griping and complaining from other parents. Hockey politics? Forget it. Not interested. "Don't approach me with stuff like that. And when people do, I'm straight up with them. I don't want to get involved. That's not what I'm here for. I'm here to watch the kids."

At first glance, pretty much everything about Katie Wakely is low-key and thoughtful. You could say the same about her two teenage boys: Dalyn, who was born in 2004, and Sid, born nineteen months after Dalyn. They both dove headfirst into hockey. Dalyn, being older, was first into the game, and almost right away, he could fly. Almost. Katie still has the video of Dalyn's first time on skates. Every once in a while, she and her husband fire it up to have a laugh. "He was wearing jeans. And he had his little shin pads just tacked right over his jeans. Dalyn's first time on skates, he was on his butt more than he was on his skates."

But it wasn't long before other parents were coming up to Katie and her husband, Jason, to tell them that Dalyn had a future in the game. Pretty soon, Dalyn was a star on pretty much every team he played for in his small town of Port Hope, an hour east of Toronto.

While Dalyn cruised through minor hockey, Sid faced some adversity. Katie says, "They've always been compared, which drives me crazy as a mom. To me, they're two completely different people, and their experiences in hockey are going to be so vastly different because they're not the same person."

Both Dalyn and Sid started out as forwards, and it seemed a perfect fit. They were scoring lots of points, and Katie says they were having fun with the game. "They really loved skating. Both boys were always scoring leaders on their teams when they were tiny. And from a young age with both of them, people were saying, 'They're going somewhere.'"

Dalyn still plays forward. But along the way, one of Sid's coaches decided Sid would be more valuable to his team playing defence. Just like that, the kid who loved to score was back on the blue line. "It was a turning point," Katie believes. And not in a good way. Sid was now playing a new position and wondering why he'd been moved. His confidence took a huge hit. Katie and Jason were at a loss as they struggled to decide how to handle it. "Because you don't know when is the right time to advocate and when is the right time to just sit back."

They decided this was a time to pull back. Sid has been playing defence ever since, and Katie has been second-guessing herself ever since. "Looking back now, I would have advocated for him more, because that, to me, was a drop in confidence that he is still recovering from."

When to push and when to pull back? Katie kept asking the question. There was never an easy answer. When Sid was on the cusp of making a higher-level team, Jason talked to the coach the night before the cuts were made and walked away feeling doubtful about Sid's chances. He wasn't keen on taking Sid to the rink for tryouts, because he didn't think Sid was going to make the team. Why put him through the misery? But this time, Katie was not prepared to pull back. "I believed in my kid and said to my husband, 'You don't have to take him, I'm going to take him. I want the coach to look me in the eye and tell me my kid is not good enough to make it. I don't want to sell him short. I want him to go out and prove that he can make it." That's what happened: Katie took Sid to the tryout, and he made the team. "It's hard to know when to push them and when not to. But I think when it's fear in the way, you kind of have to prepare them that anything can happen. You're never going to know until you try."

☙

THERE IS MUCH MORE to this story than the challenges of two boys and their parents trying to navigate the world of minor hockey. The Wakelys carry the hopes and dreams of the people of the Curve Lake First Nation, about thirty minutes north of Peterborough, Ontario. It is a small, tight-knit community where they care deeply about one another. Katie grew up in Curve Lake. Jason's roots are there. Although the boys have never lived in the community, their roots are there too. "It's nice because they have two hometowns," Katie says. "They have the friends they've made in Port Hope. And they have the support of everyone back home in Curve Lake."

Katie understands that if her boys succeed, her community will share in that success. "We've talked about the role model stuff. Both my kids take their roles pretty seriously in terms of providing a good example."

With the good comes the bad: racism. It's always lurking. When it surfaces, Katie says, it stings. "It's a really special thing to be First Nations, and just making sure that they know that, and they carry that with confidence, so that when something does happen, it's like water off a duck's back." For example, Dalyn's hair is long, an important tradition in Indigenous culture. On the ice, he sometimes hears comments, sarcastic "nice hair" stuff. Katie says he's always ready. "'You don't have anything better to say?' It doesn't bother him. He always has a comeback."

☙

Scouts loved Dalyn's game. He can score. He is physical. He is a leader. When he was eligible for the OHL draft in 2020, Katie says they expected a team to draft him in the first round. It didn't happen. "It was stressful because you hear so much leading up to the draft about where people are projecting your child to go. Hopes get up. We were told he was going to go higher."

Dalyn was taken in the second round, thirtieth overall, by the North Bay Battalion. "We don't really know what happened," Katie says. "And we've just kind of taken the stance as a family that everything happens for a reason. North Bay is where he's supposed to be."

North Bay sits on the traditional territory of the Nipissing First Nation. And right away, Dalyn's arrival as a young Indigenous hockey star sparked excitement. Several families from the First Nations community reached out to the team, offering to become Dalyn's billet family. The Wakelys were blown away.

Dalyn's new home is right on the water. "He's be able to ice fish," Katie says. "And Ski-Doo. His billets do a lot of work with First Nations kids from the community, and Dalyn has an opportunity to be a leader for them. He's all over it. He's excited." Going to North Bay and living with a First Nations family—it's almost like it was meant to be, Katie says. "If he had been drafted by a big-city team, that wouldn't have happened. We're just happy that he's where he's supposed to be."

You could say that about Sid too: he's where he's supposed to be. The year after he made the team in Quinte, he was the last cut. Katie and Sid both believe the coach got it wrong, but what can you do? This was one of the times they decided to pull back. Instead, they reached out to the AAA in Peterborough, which is just a stone's throw from Curve Lake. The coach invited Sid to a tryout. As the day approached, though, Sid wasn't so sure. He was going to take a pass. As Katie wondered if it was time to give Sid a nudge, Dalyn stepped in to do the pushing for her. "He lay in bed with him and said, 'You gotta go. Peterborough wants you. The coaches are waiting for you. They're not making a decision until you come out and skate with them.' And he went to Peterborough."

Hockey has made the family close. And in subtle ways, it has given the boys a stronger connection to their roots and their First Nations community. Every year, the boys play in the annual Little NHL friendship tournament, which draws First Nations players from across Ontario. Top players like Dalyn and Sid are put on the same team as kids who are just learning to skate. "Definitely my favourite memory," Katie says. "My kids together in the Little NHL. Because that is so rare for me. Just watching how they are with the other kids who are playing house league. And I know for Dalyn, it is a relief not to hear anything about his hair, because ninety-nine percent of the kids have long hair. Everybody is in the same boat."

THE WORRYING AND SECOND-GUESSING will never end for Katie Wakely. Did she push too much? Not enough? She has far more certainty about her main role as a hockey mom. She encourages. She supports. And she never criticizes. "They get coached enough on the ice. They don't need more coaching from you."

As a hockey mom who has struggled to get it right for her boys, Katie Wakely seems to have figured things out. Sit back. Let them play. "We're not getting any younger, and neither are they. We only have so much time with them. We might as well enjoy it."

CHAPTER 11

The Colour of Hockey

"Real change doesn't happen unless we rock this boat and unless we ruffle some feathers. That's the least of my concerns, if I'm going to make somebody upset. Even outside of hockey, I'm very committed to ensuring that our children, all children, feel safe and included."
—Lauren Camper

ALEXANDRIA BRIGGS-BLAKE HAS ALWAYS felt a connection with hockey. She grew up in a loving family in Petersburg, Virginia, a few hours south of Washington, with two older brothers who were sports fanatics. When it came time to watch TV, it was her brothers who were in charge. "I'm trying to turn on the TV to watch my cartoons, and my brothers went, 'Don't touch that television.' And my mom would be telling me they were watching TV first."

Alex started watching sports with her brothers, because really, what else could she do? Football. Boxing. Basketball. You name it. She watched it all. Somehow, hockey became a favourite. "It just intrigued me. And from that point on, I started loving sports. Living sports." She moved to Washington in her early twenties and started going to Washington Capitals games. Alex fell in love with the speed, skill, and intensity of the game.

As she got older and had kids, the love of hockey never really left her. Her two daughters learned how to skate but had no interest in their mother's sport, but her son, Antonio, knew from a young age that he wanted to be a hockey player. And Alex, of course, was all in. Antonio was two years old when he skated for the first time. Alex took him to public skating. By age four, he was pretty good on skates. That's when he turned his attention to hockey, and when Alex Briggs-Blake became a hockey mom.

It was the start of a journey that changed her life and, in so many ways, the lives of other people she touched. Alex Briggs-Blake pushed for change to make the hockey rink a more welcoming place for people of colour, including her own family. She opened doors for plenty of kids who might otherwise never have given hockey a second look.

Above everything else, Alex was a hockey mom for Antonio. His start in the sport couldn't have gone any better. Antonio signed up to play for the Fort Dupont Cannons, the longest-running minority hockey program in North America. The Cannons are run by Neal Henderson, a legend in the DC area and a US Hockey Hall of Fame member. Henderson made it his mission to get more inner-city kids onto skates and into hockey rinks. The Cannons became a snapshot of hockey's possibilities. All those life lessons taught in hockey—team-work, responsibility, and commitment—kids of colour were now part of it. Antonio had found his sport.

While her son was playing, Alex studied the Cannons hockey program. What was working there, she believed, could also work in her own neighbourhood in Prince George's County, Maryland, about a half-hour south of Washington. There was a rink not far from their home called the Tucker Road Ice Rink. Even before Antonio signed up with the Cannons, he'd taken part in one of those "try hockey" programs at his neighbourhood rink. Alex remembers it well. "He was playing football that first time he went to try hockey, and he had on his football helmet. He didn't even want to get off the ice. We literally had to say, 'Okay, it's over. We have to go.' He was four or five at the time." Antonio was the only Black kid on the ice that day. After taking in the beauty of what the Cannons were doing, and seeing all those kids finding a place in hockey, Alex wanted to do something similar in her own backyard. "That's how I started the Tucker Road Ducks. I looked at how Coach Neal did it over in DC, and that's how the vision came to me a few years later. This is what we need to do with Tucker Road, because we need a team."

She did plenty of arm twisting with local politicians. She formed partnerships with the local parks and recreation department and with the Washington Capitals. A group called Leveling the Playing Field provided the equipment to get the Ducks started. Alex became the president of the Tucker Road Parent Hockey Organization. She became a salesperson for a game that seemed to have little or no appeal to people who weren't white. "Black parents don't think of hockey as an option. If they don't see Black players out there in the NHL, at a high level or a large scale, they're not going to think about it for themselves. So I was letting them know that 'Hey, hockey is an option. Give it a shot.' Kids started signing up. We had a 'learn to play hockey for free' day, and that's how we grew our team."

As she moved forward with her plan to start up a hockey program, Alex was getting plenty of attention. She was a hockey mom who was making a difference in the lives of many. Her work helped her connect with a man named Bryant McBride, who was also trying to change hockey.

Bryant was born in Chicago. His family moved to Sault Ste. Marie, in northern Ontario, when he was young, and he took up hockey because that's what you do in the Soo. He got pretty good at it. Bryant made it as high as Junior B and stayed with hockey when he left home to get an education. He went to West Point first, then Trinity College, where he became an All-America defenceman. He was always the lone Black player. "Being called the N-word on the ice? Oh yeah, I realized it. I've never had a teammate of colour. It's crazy. What the hell is this?"

In 1994, Bryant was hired by NHL commissioner Gary Bettman to be the director of business development. He was the first Black executive to work for the league.

Bryant left the NHL in 2000 but has continued to push for change in hockey. He co-founded a program called the Carnegie Initiative, named after Black hockey great Herb Carnegie, a member of Canada's Sports Hall of Fame. Bryant's goal: to make hockey a more welcoming game. "There's lots of hope. In the next ten years, we're going to change the sport. It's an area we can change, and we will see change. We will."

It is no surprise that, through his work in hockey, Bryant has connected with others who have been pushing for change. Alex Briggs-Blake is now involved in the Carnegie Initiative, as is Lauren Camper, another hockey mom fighting for diversity at the grassroots level.

LAUREN CAMPER WAS A young girl when an older cousin collapsed on the ice and died from an undiagnosed medical condition. "So for our family, hockey held a special place in our hearts."

Years later, after Lauren got married and settled in to raise her kids, her older son, Marcel, took up roller hockey and enjoyed it. She suggested he give ice hockey a shot. When Marcel was nine, Lauren became a hockey mom. "I never really thought of becoming a hockey mom. It just kind of happened."

The Campers live in a suburb of Philadelphia. Initially, Marcel was the only Black kid in the local hockey program. Lauren became a member of the board of directors. Right away, she pushed her club to make a strong statement about diversity. "Every family should know that they are welcomed and safe. Boy, girl, gay, straight, any family should feel welcomed in the club." Her diversity statement figured prominently on the Revolution Youth Ice Hockey website.

It didn't take long for the resolve of the club to be tested on issues of race, after an incident involving Lauren's son. Marcel was in bantam at the time. Lauren says he got in a shoving match with a player on another team, who then used the N-word. Marcel's coach decided not to pursue the matter, figuring it was a minor incident that didn't escalate into much more than a couple of kids pushing and shoving. Besides, he wondered, how could you prove it?

Lauren was having none of it. "So I took matters into my own hands. At a team meeting, I took the floor and told the parents, 'If your child hears racial slurs or anything inappropriate, can you please encourage them to tell the coaches or the refs immediately? Because if they don't, it's kind of like nothing's going to happen, and nothing can happen.'"

Think how tough that would have been. The only Black mother, challenging white parents to speak up and have their children speak up. "No one wants to talk about race. It's very uncomfortable."

The following year, Marcel got into another skirmish. In the penalty box, after some jawing back and forth, the player from the other team said to Marcel, "Go back to picking cotton." Marcel's teammate heard the comment and told the coach, a different one from the year before. This time, the coach immediately went to the referee. The player who had made the racist comment was eventually suspended after Lauren went to both the league and USA Hockey. For a mother trying to protect her son, it made a difference. "I would never ignore it. I'm going to shed light on it every single time until it stops happening."

Lauren Camper got involved in the leadership of her hockey club to have a voice and make sure her voice was heard. "I'm just at a point in my life when I'm just not going to sit back and take what comes my way. If we really want to see change, we have got to call out racist behaviour when we see it so that it doesn't continue." Yet her advice for Marcel is almost the polar opposite of her actions: she tells him not to fight back. "You can't let people have power over you with words. They are words. You get them back by putting the puck in the net. That's all I've been saying to him over and over. That's how you get them back."

Her relationship with hockey is complicated. She loves so much about the game, even though she knows it's not the most welcoming sport for kids of colour. It's an especially hard sport to crack in the inner cities, where many families live in poverty. "Hockey is an expensive sport. So unless you have grants or things like that, some of those kids may never be able to touch the ice."

It's no surprise that the lives of Lauren Camper, Alex Briggs-Blake, and Bryant McBride, three powerful voices of change, would eventually intersect. "It's about being anti-racist," Bryant says. "It's about standing up and saying, 'That's wrong. Stop doing that. Cut that out.'"

Alex Briggs-Blake was making amazing progress in her efforts to build a more welcoming hockey program in her Washington suburb. The Tucker Road Ducks had become a huge success. Alex knocked on enough doors and twisted enough arms to build a program that was making hockey a viable option for a lot of families. Two hundred and fifty dollars for fees and you're in. That included equipment. Plenty of kids signed up and played hockey for the first time, many of them kids of colour.

And then the hockey rink burned down.

"It was like a second home to a lot of kids here." Alex was devastated. So were the many kids who were discovering the magic of hockey at the Tucker Road Ice Rink.

The 2017 fire was ruled accidental. The rink. The equipment. Everything was destroyed. Alex pretty much had to start from scratch. So it was back to knocking on doors and lobbying politicians for assistance to build a new rink. She also went to the NHL for financial help, and she got it. Some professional players, including Washington Capitals captain Alex Ovechkin, heard about the fire and the push to rebuild, and they stepped up too. From an awful tragedy came an outpouring of support that warms the heart of the hockey mom who made it happen. Alex Briggs-Blake's belief in hockey is now stronger than ever. "At the end of the day, it's all about kids playing a great sport."

The new Tucker Road rink cost $28 million to build. It opened in August of 2021, four years after the old rink was wiped out. The new rink includes an NHL-size ice surface, heated seats, and a dance studio. Alex's son, Antonio, had already moved on to play on a more competitive travel team by the time the new rink opened. It doesn't matter. Alex remains involved. "You have mothers who work two and three jobs. I'm like that mother who wants to support those kids. I will say this: hockey, from the NHL down, wouldn't be what it is without hockey moms."

Antonio went on to play junior hockey in New Jersey and in

Canada. He now plays college hockey in Michigan. Alex says even the ugly side of hockey has taught him valuable life lessons that will make him stronger and wiser as he goes through life. "He knows what racism is. And so, as a mother, you just say, 'You can't let what other people do, what other people say, affect you in any way, so much that it takes the joy out of what you're doing. So don't let it steal your joy. And just know that their ignorance has nothing to do with you.'"

Alex Briggs-Blake was a finalist in 2020 for the NHL's Willie O'Ree Community Hero Award for all her work with the Tucker Road Ducks hockey program. She says it was nice to be recognized, but that's not why she does what she does. "It's about the community."

Lauren Camper also keeps pushing for change to make hockey better reflect the diversity outside the rink. "Real change doesn't happen unless we rock this boat and unless we ruffle some feathers. That's the least of my concerns, if I'm going to make somebody upset. Even outside of hockey, I'm very committed to ensuring that our children, all children, feel safe and included."

These two Black hockey moms are reimagining what hockey can be. They are confident the game can get there, even if change happens one neighbourhood at a time.

CHAPTER 12

All In

"A lot of times, it's the moms making these decisions.
I think a lot of people just assumed it was my husband
making the rink and working on it every year."
—Karen Sylvester-Ceci

KAREN SYLVESTER-CECI AND HER husband, Parri, were raising their three kids in a suburb of Ottawa. There was nothing wrong with their home. But when all three kids took up hockey and she wanted to build a backyard rink for them, she discovered an issue. She had bought a "jiffy rink" from a hardware store. Peel off the top, fill it with water, let it freeze, and almost overnight, you have a backyard rink. It should have worked, she says, but it didn't. "The next morning, we woke up. We looked out the window, and the whole thing had rolled to the back of the property against the fence. We had this giant frozen sausage. I said to the kids, we're going to move."

Karen started house hunting, leaving Parri behind. She searched in the same neighbourhood so the kids could stay at the same schools, and looked for the same style of house, but without the backyard slope so she could build her rink. "When I went to see this house on a pie-shaped lot, the real estate guy says, 'Are you married?' I said yeah. 'Don't you want your husband to see the house?' I said, 'No, it's fine.'"

They checked out the kitchen first. Fine. Then they looked outside. It was dark, and the backyard was covered in snow, but Karen kept looking until she was certain the yard was flat and big enough for a hockey rink. A pool tucked in the corner was a bonus. She told the agent she would take it. He looked confused. "You don't want to look upstairs?" he asked. She didn't. She had already made up her mind. The home had a good kitchen, four bedrooms, and a pool. Most importantly for a house-hunting hockey mom, it had a backyard perfect for a rink.

Years later, the kids are grown and gone from home, and the Cecis are still in the same house. Karen Sylvester-Ceci has no regrets about her solo home-buying adventure. "A lot of times, it's the moms making these decisions. I think a lot of people just assumed it was my husband making the rink and working on it every year. It was not."

The rink was Karen's baby all the way. It was forty by sixty feet. After working a full-time job and running the kids around to rinks, after the homework and the music lessons—all of her kids played instruments—Karen would go outside and flood her rink. Sometimes it was well after midnight when she got to it.

Karen's sport when she was growing up had been figure skating. She'd spent countless hours in cold rinks, working on edge control, crosscuts, balance, and backwards skating, as well as stops and starts. Now, on her backyard rink, she put those skills to work, teaching her children proper skating techniques. She left the other hockey skills up to the fathers who coached minor hockey. Soon the neighbourhood kids began coming over, and Karen was more than happy to show them how to do forward crosscuts, pivot on their skates without losing speed, and make better transitions from forwards to backwards.

From that group of kids who showed up to play shinny and take part in Karen's impromptu skating sessions, five found their way to the NHL: Erik Gudbranson, Alan Quine, Jason Akeson, Shawn Lalonde, and Cody Ceci, one of Karen's sons. A sixth player, Joey West, played professionally in Europe. Remarkable. "It's kind of nice to see so many local kids reach their dreams," she says. "And I'm sure the extra time on the outdoor rink made a difference. Minor hockey league coaches don't always teach them to use their edges properly. I remember Cody being criticized. 'You're not skating hard enough.' But it's supposed to look effortless. You're not supposed to look like you're dying out there."

Karen was a hockey fan long before she became a hockey mom. As a teenager, she would go to junior hockey games with her friends and was enthralled by the speed of the game. The man she would marry, though, was through and through a football player. Parri Ceci was a star receiver at the University of Guelph and went on to play professionally with the CFL's Calgary Stampeders before his career was cut short by injury. He and Karen were working in the banking industry when they met and fell in love. They married and had three children. Parri had hoped his two boys would follow his lead and play football.

Karen had visions of their daughter in figure skating. It was a complete fluke that all three kids found their way to hockey instead.

Chelsea, the oldest, dove in first. She had initially followed Karen into figure skating but soon knew it wasn't her sport. By age seven, she was ready to make the jump to hockey. And she was always good. Always aggressive. "They called her the Ceci train," Karen says. "She will plow people down when she is not supposed to be hitting."

Cody followed his big sister. All those backyard drills with his mother paid off: his skating was always a thing of beauty. From early on, his game highlighted his skating and his skill. "The way he looks at it, why take a penalty when you're going to miss two minutes of a game? Why do that when you can just try to get the puck and do something smart with it?"

Cole came along five years after Cody. Almost by default, Karen says, he played hockey in a predetermined role: "They needed a goalie, so they just stuck him in the net right away in the backyard rink because they needed someone to shoot on, so Cole didn't have a choice."

It wasn't all hockey in the Ceci home. Karen and Parri set out to raise well-rounded children. All sports were encouraged. "If they wanted to try jiu-jitsu, they were in jiu-jitsu. Baseball, football, whatever they wanted." As the seasons changed, the kids changed sports. Even though all three loved playing hockey and had talent, when summer came along, Karen says, the hockey gear was tucked away until fall. She had a rule: no organized sports over the summer—that was cottage time. "Back in figure skating days, if you didn't do summer skating, you were just dying to get your skates back on in the fall. You were really looking forward to it. I used to spend my summers at the cottage, and I couldn't wait to get back on the ice in the fall. I wanted my kids to be the same way."

Playing music was another non-negotiable. "The deal was, the kids could be in any sport they wanted, but they had to play at least one instrument or be in some kind of music lesson or class." Chelsea sang and played piano before moving on to the guitar. Cody took to piano. Cole became a drummer. To this day, all three still play.

With music lessons, hockey, homework, and everything else life threw at them, the Ceci home was a busy place. Karen and Parri both worked full-time. They got plenty of help from Karen's mom, but it still wasn't enough. So they placed an ad in the local newspaper, looking for a nanny. Karen says that's when a woman named Lennie landed in her home. "She became like a grandmother to our kids. She was with us for seventeen years. She was like Mary Poppins. Amazing."

Sometimes Karen would take the bus home after work and jump right into the family van. Lennie had already loaded the kids into the van, and off they would go to the rink. "And Lennie, bless her heart, would give me a plate of dinner. And I would eat while I was driving."

All three kids were good hockey players. Chelsea was a hard-edged forward who played high-level competitive minor hockey. She eventually found an even better fit playing defence. Cole, the youngest, enjoyed his time playing net on the outdoor rink so much, he wanted to become a goaltender when he started minor hockey. His parents said no. They wanted no part of the pressure that comes with being the parents of a goaltender. They encouraged Cole to play defence.

And he did. He won a city championship when he was ten. But then, on his own, he decided that was it for defence. "He went and shook his coach's hand and said, 'Thank you very much. But I'm not going to be back next year.'" He told the coach he had decided to become a goaltender. "We let him do it," Karen says, but she and Parri were thinking, "He's going to get a million shots on him, and he's going to hate it." They were wrong. "He's still a goalie now. And he loves it." Cole ended up playing three years in the OHL, then moved on to play for York University.

Sandwiched in the middle was Cody, whose smooth skating always made him stand out. Even so, Karen never imagined he would go on to have a long career in the NHL. She remembers one coach who, early on, pulled the parents together and set out realistic expectations for a new season. It was a message parents needed to hear. "He said, 'We're going to learn teamwork. We're going to have fun. We're going to learn some skills. But I'm not here to make NHL players out of your kids.'" He outlined the nearly impossible odds of ever playing a game in the NHL. "That made me realize how slim a chance it was that this could actually happen."

Cody was determined to be the kid who beat the odds. He clung to his dreams of playing in the NHL. He was a quiet, hard-working kid who kept getting better and developed into a solid two-way defence-man. For the most part, his was a smooth hockey journey. By the time he reached his teens, junior scouts were taking notice.

He was playing AA in Ottawa at age thirteen when another parent talked to Karen and Parri about the prestigious Lakefield College

School, near Peterborough, Ontario, a private school that seemed perfect for Cody's style of learning. Karen and Parri took Cody for a visit. "We knew we couldn't afford it and said, 'Thanks, but no thanks' at the end of the tour," she says. But Cody was sold. The school was everything he could have imagined. There were just six students in each class. And climbing walls. And an outdoor rink with a Zamboni. It was along the water. It would be like going to school at a private cottage. Karen says it was perfect; they just needed a way to make it work. "So we applied for a bursary and ended up getting it. Cody was accepted and registered to join the school that fall."

Cody's life quickly got complicated. He was set to play minor hockey in Peterborough, a half-hour from school, when out of the blue he was told no. "They were playing their first pre-season tournament in Ottawa, and it got challenged by the coach of the Eastern Ontario Wild major bantam team. They took Cody off the ice, and he wasn't allowed to play hockey." Hockey Canada rules require young players to play in their home jurisdiction. The rule is there to keep teams from recruiting top players and stacking teams. Cody's family argued that his home was now his boarding school in Lakefield and that he had left home for educational purposes. The hearings and appeals took months. Finally, Cody was given permission to play minor hockey in Peterborough. But for four months, his career had been sidelined. "All he wanted to do was play," Karen says. "It drove me crazy. It went all the way up to Hockey Canada before it was resolved. He was ready to quit hockey at that point. Finally, they agreed to let him play."

That time away from hockey was tough for both mother and son. "It didn't make sense to him. He went to a different school, and all of a sudden, he couldn't play hockey. He keeps everything inside. That worries me all the time."

Cody Ceci spent two years at Lakefield College School. Other than those awful first few months without hockey, it was a great experience for him. By the time his OHL draft year came along, there was no doubt that he could have a career in junior hockey if he wanted it.

His mother wanted no part of junior hockey. She hoped Cody would go the US college route and get a good education while playing top-level hockey. Eventually, they struck a deal: if an OHL team chose Cody in the first round, he'd decide where he would play hockey; if he was picked after the first round, Karen and Parri would decide.

That 2009 draft was stressful, Karen remembers. "He was away at school. He's watching the draft on his laptop. I was home watching it on mine. Parri was in Montreal with Cole at a tournament, watching on his laptop." Cody Ceci was chosen in the first round by his hometown team, the Ottawa 67's. "As exciting as it was, having to leave Lakefield was tough on him. But having the family back together was great. I thought when he left home at thirteen, I was not going to see him at home again," Karen says. "To get chosen by the 67's—what are the chances that he'd get drafted back home to Ottawa?" If she had concerns about Cody not going to college, they disappeared quickly. "It worked out well, fortunately. It doesn't work out well often, right?"

Cody spent almost four full seasons with the 67's. Karen says it was four nearly perfect years. "It was surreal. It was so exciting to go to those games. It was a really fun experience. The whole family would go. Both grandmothers. It was great."

Playing junior hockey for his hometown team was magical. And it got even better in 2012, Cody's NHL draft year. His entire family made the trip to Pittsburgh for the draft. Once again, he was a first-round draft pick. And once again, Cody Ceci was chosen by a team from Ottawa. He had become a junior star at home. Now, he would launch his NHL career with the Ottawa Senators.

Bryan Murray, the general manager who had drafted Cody, caught up with Karen and Cody soon after the draft. "He said to Cody, 'You're so lucky. You live in Ottawa and you can come to our rink and work out all summer.'" Karen stepped in right away. "'No, no. We have this hockey rule. We go to the cottage.' Bryan just looked at me and smiled and said, 'You know, back in the day, when hockey ended, I'd go to my cottage, and I wouldn't come back to the rink until training camp started. Now they expect me to be there every day.'"

Cody listened to the conversation between his mom and his new general manager and said nothing. He didn't have to. "Cody was just staring at me, and I knew I had to stop talking."

The cottage time continued for Cody, but not as frequently. Both the 67's and the Senators provided Cody with a workout routine, and Karen says he followed it religiously. They set up a temporary gym underneath a ten-by-twenty-foot canopy. "If he had to run wind sprints, he was doing it on a road behind the cottage. Ice time meant returning to the city. Nobody takes the summer off. It doesn't happen anymore."

Cody landed in the NHL to stay when he was just nineteen years old. He played his first NHL game in his hometown. When it was over, Cody met with an army of friends and family who were there to watch—including the minor hockey coach who had told his parents that NHL dreams were unrealistic. "He came to Cody and said 'I have to apologize,'" Karen remembers. "He said, 'I actually told your parents I wasn't going to make an NHL player out of you. I lied.'" Right away, it hit home for Karen how many people had helped Cody reach the NHL.

CODY WAS THRILLED THAT he was starting his NHL career playing for his hometown team—the team he grew up cheering for. He soon realized the pressures of the NHL are even more intense when you play in a Canadian market. In those early days, Karen, too, was discovering that playing in the NHL can be unforgiving. "It's really bad. The thing that drives me crazy, you would think your local sports media people would try to support their own team, their hometown team. But to bash these players on the radio while these guys are driving to their own game, it's horrible. They don't need the whole world telling them that they're having a tough time right now. They know it. I hate that part of it."

She had run a Twitter account on behalf of the Ottawa 67's during Cody's junior career and enjoyed it. But after seeing so many negative comments about her son after he turned pro, Karen is now off social media. And when she is in her car, she listens to anything but sports radio. "People at work will say, 'How do you feel about what they said about Cody?' I say, 'I don't even know what they said.' He doesn't either. At the end of the day, the only opinions that matter are the coach's, the general manager's, and the player's. So why pay attention to the rest?"

When the pressures of hockey become too great, Cody turns to music. All those lessons when he was a kid made him a pretty good piano player. When he began his pro career in the AHL, his parents gave him an electronic piano so he could keep playing.

There was one magical run for the Ottawa Senators during Cody's time with the team. It was 2017. The Senators were one game away from playing in the Stanley Cup Final. The pressure was immense. In the middle of the night, Cody couldn't sleep and texted his mother. "I thought, 'Oh my god, something's wrong.' I grabbed my phone and had a look." There was nothing wrong. Cody had wandered down to a hotel ballroom in Pittsburgh. There, he found a grand piano and started playing. And that's when he texted his mom, saying, "The acoustics are amazing here. I think I need to get a carpet in my music room at home."

Music has never been far from his heart, his mother says. "It just relaxes him. Helps him de-stress after a game. He loves it." In fact, music remains important to all her kids. "At the cottage in the summer, they've got a rock band going. Cody on piano. Chelsea plays guitar and sings, and Cole plays drums. They love music."

Her kids are adults now. Chelsea, who is a few years older than Cody, is still playing recreational hockey. Cole, the youngest, has given Karen the experience she never wanted: she is a goalie mom. And it's every bit as bad as she thought it would be. "It's awful. I was never ever nervous at a game until he went into net. Now I am a complete wreck. If he goes into a shootout, I have to physically leave the rink and have someone text me and tell me what happened. It's awful."

As she watches Cole play at York University, she often thinks back to those days when he was stopping pucks for his brother and sister. "As busy as we were, going to all those games and practices, they'd get home at eleven o'clock sometimes and head out to our backyard rink because they just loved being there. I'd have to pull them off the ice at midnight or one and say, 'You guys, you've got school tomorrow.'"

So many wonderful memories. Looking back, Karen says she wouldn't change a thing. "I think our role as parents is to support them as much as we can. To enable their dreams. Don't force them to play hockey because there may be a chance they will play in the NHL. Don't be like that. Be supportive and let them try different things. Our job is to get them there. And to pick up the pieces if they have a bad game."

CHAPTER 13

Transferable Skills

"Those skills in hockey are really transferable skills to everyday life. Team-
work. Staying back and letting somebody else take the puck and do some-
thing. That kind of steady persistence and teamwork and reliability. And
you're always trying to be better and trying to learn new things."
—Gloria Sobb

WHEN HER TWO YOUNG boys told her they wanted to play hockey, Gloria Sobb had no interest. She would come around; she had no choice. Her older son, Matt, was first. Marty followed two years later. In those early days, it was so easy to get sucked into the sport. "It was cute. They were wobbly. Then they got their hockey sticks, and they could kind of lean on their sticks and skate down the ice, and they loved that."

Her boys were having a ball, and Gloria was thrilled watching it. "They were four or five and their shirts were down to their knees. They'd skate two steps and fall on their bums. Like, we loved everything they did. They'd put ten pucks on the ice, and ten kids would go scrambling after them. We thought it was fabulous."

Matt and Marty were decent hockey players, but they were never destined to be stars. For the most part, the boys played in good, dependable house leagues. Gloria was fine with that. "They loved it. Absolutely loved it. There was no pressure. They were good, but they were never the stars of the show."

It was, in many ways, hockey at its purest. No great expectations. No real pressure. "None of them were going to the NHL," Gloria says. "So they just had fun. And I had fun. I enjoyed my time in the stands with my friends whose kids were on the same team. And I don't remember too many real disagreements in the stands. Everyone was pretty good."

At her boys' house league games, there were no noisemakers or cowbells. "I remember this one mother stood up. The arena was quiet. And she yelled out 'Skate. Skate.' And someone says, 'What do you think they're out here for? Fresh air and exercise?'" In so many ways, she says, it was what minor hockey should be. "I remember how proud we were when they did well. And they were just beaming if they made a good play or scored a goal."

By the time Matt and Marty hit their teen years, they were pretty much done with hockey. They dabbled in music. They became skiers. Their mother looks back on their hockey years now with no regrets. "It was really good for them. I think it taught them teamwork. It taught them responsibility. All the good things you want to teach your kids; it was easy to do through hockey."

As the boys got older, those life lessons took on new meaning as they dove deeper into the music world. Cody Ceci's mom says if Cody hadn't made it in hockey, he probably would have turned to music. Matt and Marty Sobb took the alternate road and became musicians. The lessons they learned on the hockey rink became the template for success in music.

Marty showed the earliest interest in music. He played guitar in a high school band he had started, and they needed a drummer. He reached out to his older brother, Matt, who was raw but talented. Matt kept drumming as he began university. After his first semester, he told his mom he was quitting school to play music. "He said, 'It's only temporary, Mom. I'm going to do it for a year, then go back to school.' That didn't happen."

Decades later, Matt is still playing the drums. In fact, he has made a living playing music his entire adult life. Since 2008, he has been the drummer for the band MonkeyJunk, one of the top blues bands in Canada. MonkeyJunk has won two JUNO awards and has played on stages around the world. Marty also makes a living in the music world, as a sound engineer at a recording studio. He has also developed into a gifted musician.

Her boys' success in music, Gloria says, was without a doubt helped along by their experiences playing hockey. "Those skills in hockey are really transferable skills to everyday life. Teamwork. Staying back and letting somebody else take the puck and do something. As a drummer, you're always in the background. But there wouldn't be any music without the drummer. That kind of steady persistence and teamwork and reliability. And you're always trying to be better and trying to learn new things."

Matt has renewed his passion for hockey, playing often with a bunch of musicians. He has been a regular in the Juno Cup, a charity game in which former NHLers line up against musicians.

And Gloria Sobb, the one-time hockey mom, is now a long-time musician mom. She enjoys every minute of it. "I'm very proud of both of them. The best part, I think, is that they're nice kids. They are helpful. And they're fair, and they're just kind. They're kind kids."

CHAPTER 14

Far-North Hockey

"The kids all shared. Older kids. Younger kids. Your turn to shovel,
you shovelled. You can come and go as you please. Stay as long
as you want. And there is no pressure."
—Trina Daigneault

TRINA DAIGNEAULT, a hockey mom and hockey coach, grew up and still lives in Hay River in the Northwest Territories. It bills itself as the place where the arctic adventure begins. It's hard to argue with that. An eleven-hour drive north from Edmonton will put you on the southern shores of Great Slave Lake and at the town of Hay River, where they fish, they hunt and, in the winter, they play hockey.

Trina didn't play hockey growing up. She was of a generation when it wasn't even an option for her. "Girls figure skated, boys played hockey. Not that I wanted to play hockey."

Her two children, Michelle and Luke, like many kids in Hay River, had their first skating lessons on an outdoor rink. "It was great for after supper, because they could burn off some energy before they went to bed. They were all cold. So you get them home in a hot tub. Toasty. Then into bed. It was great."

Trina would take her kids to their skating lessons and shake her head as she watched. "They were all volunteers, and they were really good at teaching hockey but not at teaching how to skate. I thought, 'I can help and teach the kids how to skate properly and help them with their hockey.' That's how I got involved. I switched my figure skates for hockey skates."

She was new to hockey, but she was about to learn. Her community needed hockey coaches. She agreed to help. "I took some training and got my level one coaching certification. My husband was probably my best resource for hockey. I'd come home and say, 'Okay, I have this problem. What do I do?' And he would explain it to me so I could explain it to the kids."

She saw how hockey brought her community together, especially at the outdoor rink. "Every evening we would go to the rink at five thirty. The kids all shared. Older kids. Younger kids. Your turn to shovel, you shovelled. You can come and go as you please. Stay as long as you want. And there is no pressure."

Trina coached Michelle for a while, then moved over to coach Luke. Both developed into strong players. "We notice our teams have lots of skills. It's because they have three hours of practice ice time a week. They get to work on their skills a lot. Where our players fall down a lot, they don't have game experience. They don't have competition."

When you barely have the numbers to scrape together a team or two in each age group, it's hard to develop balanced competition. It wasn't unusual to see games become one-sided. When that happened, Trina wasn't happy. "The game has to be fun for everyone. Sometimes when I was coaching Luke, I'd get upset with him because he was scoring too many goals. We're winning. We didn't need to be winning by ten."

Michelle played on a boys' travelling team. With the closest town three hours away, weekends were spent on frozen northern highways. Trina says Michelle had loads of talent and wanted desperately to see where it could take her. "She had a friend who was at a hockey academy in Alberta. She came to us and said, 'Can I do this? Can we make it happen?'"

Michelle was fourteen years old when she left home. "It was tough," her mother remembers. "There were a lot of tears when she left. It's what she wanted to be doing, right? But it was still hard." She played for two winters in Edmonton, staying with a billet family. It was a difficult adjustment for a young Inuk girl who had grown up in a small, protected environment. For the first time in her life, Michelle was confronted with racism, in the form of comments written by teammates. "They were horrible. Racist. And disappointing. I asked her if she wanted me to talk to the coaches. She did not want me to; it would just create more troubles. Michelle figured they were just jealous of her abilities and what she was able to accomplish. She figured it just wasn't worth it." Trina and her husband stayed on the sidelines, trusting their daughter's decision. Michelle sat down with some of the people involved and dealt with the racism issues on her own. Still, Trina says, "There were times you knew it was happening and felt helpless about trying to get it resolved or help her avoid the bullying."

For the most part, the support Michelle received in her hockey journey was overwhelming. She competed in the National Aboriginal Hockey Championships, playing in front of hockey scouts from across the country. She was recruited to play AA in Ottawa and played on the same team as Chelsea Ceci. Karen Sylvester-Ceci became Michelle's billet mom. She was among four billet moms that Trina came to rely on to look after her daughter as she chased her hockey dreams. "We started joking about Michelle having these 'winter moms.' I knew she would always be okay with these people. We always knew the winter moms would have her back home safely at the end of the season."

Michelle's hockey path finally carried her to the women's hockey team at McGill University in Montreal. She is now teaching grade school in Montreal. "She has made friends all across the country," her mother says. "And she has stayed in contact with them. It has been phenomenal."

Trina Daigneault knows it took courage for her daughter to leave home at such a young age to see where hockey could take her. And she made it. "She worked for everything she got. She earned it."

CHAPTER 15

Goalie Moms: A Special Breed

"There's a bigger picture that I'm not part of that involves the team and what goes on with that team. My job is to stay out of that. My focus was on supporting him. That meant being an asset to him instead of getting in the way."
—Sue Taylor

SUE TAYLOR SAYS WITH absolute certainty that her son Seamus Kotyk was born to be a goaltender. "He would be running around the house in diapers. And he would give you a ball so you could shoot it at him. He didn't want to play Lego or Fisher-Price or anything. He wanted you to shoot something at him."

Seamus became a good goaltender over time. He had an outstanding junior career, and in 1999, he was drafted by the Boston Bruins. Sue was with him at the draft. And she was with him several years later when he got his one and only call-up to the NHL. By then, Seamus was part of the San Jose Sharks organization and a member of the Sharks' top farm team, the Cleveland Barons. Seamus was in net one night in November as the Barons played in Toronto against the AHL's Toronto Marlies. His mom was at that game. She and her older son, Kyle, had made the two-hour drive from their home in London, Ontario. And it wasn't pretty. "In my opinion, as a mom, it was not one of his better games. And I kept thinking, 'Is it because we're here watching him play?'"

After the game, Seamus found his mother. And he was smiling. "Ma," he said. "I've been called up."

One of the goaltenders in San Jose had been injured. Seamus got the call to be the backup and spent seven games with the Sharks. There was a hope, almost an expectation, that he would get to play in his first NHL game. It never happened. In his eight seasons of professional hockey, that was the closest he would come to playing in the NHL. After all the hard work, and sacrifice, to come so close . . .

His mom has no regrets. "For me, and maybe I'm weird, playing on the ice in the NHL was never the end. That was never the objective. There were smaller objectives along the way to get there." The hockey journey is what mattered most to Sue Taylor. That's why, when she reflects on her son's career, there are no 'what ifs' in the back of her mind. "As far as I'm concerned, hey, he dressed for an NHL team."

SUE TAYLOR GREW UP in a hockey family. Her father attended Boston Bruins training camps in the late 1940s. "I mean, I grew up in northern Ontario. So everybody knew hockey. And everybody knew bingo. Those were the two staples of what we did."

She got married and had two boys, two years apart. Seamus, the younger son, was just a toddler when Sue became a single mom. Money was tight at times, but Sue and her young family always got by. "Goalie pads and skates are not cheap, never mind winter jackets and boots." Her father was always good to help, slipping the kids a twenty now and then. "He'd say, 'A man's always got to have a couple of bucks in his pocket.'"

Hockey became the sport that kept Sue and her sons going. She built a backyard rink the year she bought her first house, and away they would go for hours and hours. The boys helped her maintain the rink. "I'm not saying our rink was the best ever. But it was our rink."

Kyle played hockey for a while. "He was a good defenceman," his mom says. But Kyle had nowhere near the passion for the game that Seamus had. "Hockey was not going to be his life. Life was going to be his life. He's interested in absolutely everything. So his involvement with sports was downhill skiing and then high school football." For Seamus, on the other hand, "His whole life was hockey . . . hockey and nothing else."

Seamus was a good athlete, and all that time he spent on outdoor rinks made him a terrific skater. Sue says, "I'm not a skills and performance trainer, but I would say he is one of the smoothest skaters I have ever seen. You'd see some kids working and working. He just put the skates on and he was gone."

He played other positions for a while. And maybe he could have made it as a forward or defenceman. But no, Seamus was hell-bent on being a goalie. Sue soon discovered that the life of a goalie's mom isn't easy. "I had a hard time sitting. And I kept to myself as much as I could."

Seamus made life easier on his mom because he was skilled at stopping pucks. Bad goals or bad games were rare. When he struggled, his mom says, he rarely needed to be told what he had done wrong. "That, to me, was one of his most outstanding characteristics: his level of self-awareness and self-intuition from a very young age. It was remarkable. We would have conversations, and I would honestly think, 'Who is the parent here?' His attention to detail and situational assessment were off the charts. And I frequently had times when I was thinking, 'I need to take this even more seriously if I'm going to continue to support and nurture him.' Because he was coming at it from a level that I hadn't even considered."

Plenty of parents and young hockey players dread the drive home after a bad game. Sue says that was never the case with Seamus. She would start a conversation by pointing out some positives from what she had seen. And then she would ask questions, not to be critical but to better understand things. "I would say, 'At the six-minute mark of the second period, did you notice that defenceman on the other team?' And he did. What intrigued me was, at fourteen, he could remember the six-minute mark of the second period. Because that was his life."

Her goal with both boys was to give them every opportunity to make it in life. By the time Seamus was a teenager, Sue felt it was time to move away from Sault Ste. Marie, to give him more opportunities in hockey. She has always been self-employed, being brought in by companies and governments as a skills training expert, which gave her the flexibility to pack up and move. And that's what they did. They moved to southern Ontario, where Seamus played Junior B and Junior A for a few years. Different coaching. More scouts around. Sue has no doubts that the move south was beneficial.

Seamus was sixteen years old when he was drafted by the Ottawa 67's of the OHL. He made the team that first season and was on his way to establishing himself as one of the best junior goaltenders in the country. He led his team to a Memorial Cup championship in his second season. A few months later, he was drafted by the Boston Bruins. His mother was thrilled. "I said, 'Oh my god, your grandfather attended their training camp.' I thought that was cool. I thought it was just amazing to be there."

He would be back at the Memorial Cup playoffs during the last of his four junior seasons, in 2001. His team didn't win that year, but Seamus was a standout.

It was a solid junior career. Sue went to as many of his games as she could. "I spent four years driving down a highway. My whole life was about getting to a game on time. And not looking like I had just driven seven hours." When she wasn't there in person, she would watch on TV or listen to the radio.

In early 2000, Sue was trying to watch on her computer while Seamus was in net in a game against the Hull Olympiques. It was the early days of the Internet, and her screen kept freezing, so she was having a hard time following the game. "And all of a sudden, the announcer says, 'Our goalie is down, our goalie is down.'"

It was Seamus. Out of the blue, while waiting for a faceoff, he had blacked out and collapsed just in front of his net. He wasn't moving, and inside the rink there was both panic and silence.

By now, Sue was feeling panicked. She still didn't know why, though she had good reason to fear the worst. "The camera didn't go to Seamus. I had no cellphone in those days. Do I stay online and watch for information? But what if someone is trying to call me?" She stayed online for a bit. She heard the game was being cancelled. She could see Seamus being taken away on a stretcher. It was every mother's nightmare.

Kyle had made the trip to Hull to watch the game. He borrowed a phone from a rink attendant and called his mom. "All he said was, 'Mom, his lips are blue. He's passed out on the ice.'" She told Kyle to find Seamus and stay with him. "He said, 'There are people telling me I can't.' I said, 'You don't leave your brother.'" But Kyle couldn't make it past security. And he wasn't able to be with Seamus as he was loaded into an ambulance and taken to hospital. It seemed like an eternity before Sue finally got a call from Seamus's billet mom, who said Seamus was conscious and doing alright.

Sue's immediate concern was her son's heart. Earlier that season, doctors had treated Seamus for a heart defect. He had been feeling sluggish before the season. He went for a checkup and, just like that, he was at the Heart Institute in Ottawa. That episode had caught his mother off guard. "There was no history. Nothing. This was the kid who wasn't sick. Healthy and stubborn his whole life." And now, after a long and cautious recovery, he had passed out cold on the ice. His mother debated: Drive to Ottawa overnight? Or fly out the next morning? It was a long and difficult night as she waited to catch a morning flight.

It turned out Seamus Kotyk was suffering from exhaustion that night in Hull. That's why he collapsed. Still, as a precaution, he didn't play the rest of that season. Rather than return home to London with his mother, Seamus remained in Ottawa with his billet family. "My instinct was to bring him home. That's not what he needed. He was part of a team, and he wanted to remain in Ottawa with his team."

He came back the next year with plenty to prove because the questions about his health were still out there. The Bruins never signed him to a contract, but the San Jose Sharks organization eventually came calling, and Seamus didn't disappoint. He put together a solid career in the AHL. In 2005, he became just the eighth goaltender in league history to score a goal. He closed out his playing career with a few seasons in Europe. Before he reached his thirtieth birthday, he was done, ready to move on to a new career.

Since 2009, Seamus has been coaching and developing players. He is now the goaltending development coach of the Buffalo Sabres. His brother, Kyle, has built a career as a chartered accountant. Sue says, "It was far more important to me that my sons grow up to be good men than it was for them to be good hockey players."

Hockey was always a challenge for Sue, in large part because Seamus played the most unforgiving position in the game. When emotions ran high in games and among other parents, she would simply walk away, to be by herself. "I can regroup. So watching a game by myself helped me. I could have conversations with myself." She decided early on to stay out of it when Seamus wasn't seeing much ice time. "Of course, if your kid doesn't play, you're not happy. But there's a bigger picture that

I'm not part of that involves the team and what goes on with that team. My job is to stay out of that. My focus was on supporting him. That meant being an asset to him instead of getting in the way."

And always there were the other parents. Sue says you can choose your friends, but you can't choose your hockey family. "I met a family when he was very young that today are still my close friends. There are some really good people that I met. The others, you just say, 'Hello. How are you?'"

Both Seamus and Sue hoped he would play in the NHL. But hockey, she believes, never did define who Seamus was. Maybe that explains why one moment from his call-up to San Jose remains a favourite memory. When Seamus got the call to join the Sharks, Sue immediately upgraded her TV package to avoid missing a minute. And when the warm-ups began, there was her son, dressed from head to toe in the teal of the San Jose Sharks. At that moment, Sue Taylor, a proud hockey mom, couldn't help herself. "And you know what I did? This is classic mother. I called him on his cellphone. And, of course, he changed his message. He sounded so grown up and official. I was really proud of him. And I said, 'Seamus, you look so good on TV.' And because I had done seven years of postdated cheques for braces, I said to him, 'You smile at the camera, and you show everybody how nice your teeth are.'"

Seamus called his mom after the game. It was moments after his first time on an NHL bench during a regular-season game. "And he said to me, 'Ma, don't go leaving me messages like that anymore.'"

Sue Taylor laughs as she tells that story. And she is proud when she looks back at a kid who loved hockey and found a way to make a career out of it. "He had a good career. All the things that were important to him personally and as a professional hockey player—he hit those markers. And he looked damn good in teal."

CHAPTER 16

He's a '91

"The best player? No. The best skill player? Tons of people are better.
The most devoted, dedicated, and hard-working player?
Well, you could probably put him pretty close to the top."
—Darlene Shaw

CHRIS DUCHENE, THE MOTHER of veteran NHL forward Matt
Duchene, knew almost from the day Matt was born that he was going
to be a hockey player. "My husband and I were hockey crazy, and Matt
was born in that environment." Matt was on skates at eighteen months,
and there was no turning back.

Chris was raised in a hockey family. Her four brothers all played.
Two were drafted by NHL teams. One of her brothers, Newell Brown,
has been an NHL assistant coach for more than three decades. Matt's
father, Vince, played juvenile hockey. They have lived hockey. They
understand it.

Initially, for Matt, it was hockey in the winter and everything else in the summer, including plenty of street hockey. He really did love the game. As much as Chris tried to introduce her son to many different sports, Matt was having none of it. "It was always hockey, hockey, hockey," his mother says. "Drove a lot of people crazy."

The skating skills that are so apparent in his game now didn't happen by accident. "He wasn't a very good skater, but my husband has a great knack for understanding what skills are important. We worked on skating wherever we could." Chris and Vince enrolled their son in CanSkate lessons with a figure skating instructor, who gave Matt a program to follow. Chris says Matt was diligent. "He had a passion, a drive, a willingness to improve all the time. We didn't have to say, 'Okay, tonight you have to do this. You have to work hard.' Just right from the beginning, he had a motivation to get better. And that was internal."

Chris worked full-time at the public high school in Haliburton, Ontario, for over thirty years, eventually becoming the head of the guidance department. She retired in 2020, her thirty-eighth year in teaching, and is now a supply teacher. "I didn't take any time off. I didn't even take full-time maternity leave with my kids. I loved my job." Her only other child, a younger daughter, Jess, was also involved in sports, as a figure skater and high school hockey player. Her husband worked in real estate, and Matt played hockey non-stop, with plenty of travel. It was busy. "You're young, and you have all that energy to do all the things you have to do. It's great, your hockey journey with the kids."

❧

AROUND THE SAME TIME, a similar story was evolving for Darlene Shaw, a hockey mom in Belleville, Ontario, a few hours southeast of where Chris Duchene was raising her family.

Andrew Shaw, the third of four Shaw children, was born in 1991, making him part of the same hockey cohort and draft year as Matt Duchene. Long before she became a hockey mom to a future NHL player, Darlene Shaw was a hockey fan. "My father brought me to a Junior B game when I was six or seven. And I loved it from the get-go."

Sports was everything in the Shaw household. Hockey dominated. Alexandria, the oldest, got into figure skating. The three boys came next, first Josh, then Andrew, and finally Jason, and they all played hockey. The Shaws built a tiny backyard rink that did the trick, and that's where the kids learned to skate.

Andrew was four years old when he started skating lessons with his brother Jason, who is just thirteen months younger. When they were on the ice together, their mother was right there with them. "I remember the coach saying, 'Mrs. Shaw, you don't have to be out here.' I'd say, 'Yeah, I do.' Then the instructor would say, 'Okay, I understand.' They both went, and they ran and ran, and they couldn't stop. So they'd run into the boards, or they'd run into each other. And I'd usually have to stop them before they ran into somebody else."

Andrew Shaw loved everything about hockey. And he pushed himself to improve. But was he a natural? His mom says not even close. "The best player? No. The best skill player? Tons of people are better.

The most devoted, dedicated, and hard-working player? Well, you could probably put him pretty close to the top."

Both Darlene and her husband coached hockey when the boys were young. In fact, Darlene coached Andrew and his younger brother in tyke hockey. But Darlene's involvement was short-lived. "Most of the parents were great. But there were a few who drove me to quit."

The style of hockey that would launch Andrew Shaw to the NHL and help him become an important piece on two Stanley Cup teams was being developed almost from the first time he laced on skates. He would sweat and grind and almost will himself to succeed. He was, his mom says, that kid who never quit. "We worked hard all our lives. We've never been in big-paying jobs. But we've worked our butts off to get what we have and to give them what they have. They've seen that. And they know they are not the most skilled, but they can make up for it by being the hardest worker."

Darlene spent twenty years working as a bookkeeper for a taxi company, then moved on to a trucking company. She knows hard work. "I usually worked eight till four. Most hockey stuff didn't start till five, so I could get home and get organized."

Between Alex and her figure skating and the three boys with their hockey, it was busy. "There was a Crock-Pot. We always tried to sit down. We always tried to have a proper meal. Meat and potatoes most of the time." Mix in school, and the house got even busier. None of her kids were scholars. And for Darlene, getting them to complete assignments was a challenge. "Once they hit high school, I had to sit right on them to do it. It is hard when they didn't want to be there. There were times I had to sit on them because they would wrestle or whatever. It drove other people crazy. Didn't drive me crazy."

Darlene was bringing in money. So was her husband, Doug, who ran his own small construction company. Still, with four kids in sports, she says, the money was always tight. "We got full sponsorship for all our kids. We had a wonderful set of friends who would sponsor us through their businesses and stuff like that and help us. Usually, you could raise fifteen hundred dollars a year towards their fees. And we did that. I had a guy ask me to keep track of all my expenses over a year. After a month, I quit because it made me sick."

For much of his minor hockey career, Andrew was coached by his father, an old-school hockey guy. Darlene says what Doug wanted more than anything from his players was an honest effort. "Your parents paid all this money. You have to give us your best every single time you're out here." Doug pretty much got what he wanted from his own kids. They never really had to have a conversation about effort at home. The three Shaw boys were all heart and soul. The boys loved playing. Doug loved coaching. And Darlene was often involved as a team manager.

Looking back, Darlene can think of only one time when she wondered if hockey might not be the best fit. She was managing Andrew's team in Belleville, but too much bickering from the parents was wearing her down. "I was like, I can't do this. I'm not a bad person, but they try to make you feel like you're a bad person." That's when she sat down with her three boys and suggested that they pack in hockey and take up skiing as a family. "It was Andrew who spoke up and said, 'But I love hockey.'"

They didn't abandon hockey. Instead, they transferred to a neigh-bouring minor hockey association. It meant longer drives to get to games, but that was a small price to pay to rediscover the joy that was being sucked out of the game.

Darlene and Doug pulled back from coaching and volunteering. She says the change made a huge difference. "We'd just go and watch our boys play, and that was an awesome year."

The boys were all good players, but they were never the stars of their teams. That includes Andrew, the future NHL player. Not once during his minor hockey career did Darlene look at him and think, "Here is a kid who is going to make it." Instead, she says, "He had to work for everything he got."

By THE TIME THEY reached bantam, Andrew Shaw and Matt Duchene still hadn't crossed paths. That was about to change. They had just become teenagers when they faced each other in an exhibition game. Darlene Shaw says before, during, and after the game, everyone was raving about Matt Duchene. He was going to be that kid who makes it, people were saying. And the exhibition game only confirmed the hype. "Thirteen to two or something. Matt had like nine or ten points. And Doug was like, 'Oh my, this kid is amazing.'"

The Shaws had no way of knowing that all that skill was the product of hard work. And despite the style differences between the two future NHL players, deep down, there were many similarities between their families.

Matt Duchene was seven years old when his parents took him to play AAA hockey with the Central Ontario Wolves. His home games and practices were more than an hour from home. Sometimes, when the weather was nasty, Chris would suggest to Matt that he take a night off. The answer was always no. "Matt always wanted to go. That was my red flag gauge on the whole thing from the beginning. Like, if this kid ever said 'I don't want to go,' then we're done."

Those long car rides several nights a week turned out to be some of Chris's favourite hockey memories. The whole family went, including Jess. "There were so many good talks in the car. Even my daughter gained so much as a little girl, listening. I mean, you do the hockey stuff, but you also talk about how to be a good friend and how to be a good teammate. And how to be kind and treat people with respect. You do all that talking in the car with a captive audience, because we had hours in the car."

They talked. The kids did homework. And the family became close. "A lot of people to this day don't understand how close we are with our kids. I think it just started with that; so much time in a car and doing so much stuff as a family."

Matt worked hard at his skating, and it got better. Along the way, his game got better too. By the time he played that exhibition game against Andrew Shaw's team in bantam, he was a star on his team. And his mother says he was still pushing to get better. "He was very passionate about it."

So what do you do with a kid this good who is ripping it up in a small town? That was the question his parents asked. Chris's first step was taking a more active role in Matt's off-ice practices. She had always been an advocate of healthy eating and proper training. "I researched a lot into when he should start training and how we were going to do that in a local community where there was no personal training."

One season, Matt fractured his collarbone. A year later he broke his leg. Both times, Chris set up his rehab programs. "We called it rehabbing like a pro. We read everything there was to read about healing quicker." She bought special equipment to accelerate his recovery. She monitored what Matt ate. "We took on every challenge with a positive attitude, like, let's do this like you do everything else, and do the best you can do."

The year he was to be drafted into junior hockey, Matt suffered another major setback. He was a high school track athlete and threw his back out throwing a discus. "He was bent over like an old man. Couldn't even walk." By then, there was an athletic therapist in town. Chris got her son in, then helped him get back on his feet. Within a couple of months, Matt was back playing hockey.

Matt's health was obviously a concern for Chris. So was his education. She found ways for him to catch up on his sleep so school didn't suffer. "I made sure school was a habit for Matt. It was non-negotiable." It was always her goal to give Matt the opportunity to chase his hockey dreams playing at a Canadian university or a US college.

BOTH MATT DUCHENE AND Andrew Shaw were drafted by OHL teams in 2007. Matt Duchene was taken in the first round, fifth overall, by the Brampton Battalion. Andrew Shaw hung around until round eleven and was drafted by the Mississauga IceDogs.

Matt played right away for Brampton. He was fifteen years old when he left home. Chris always believed that kids mature quicker with some independence. She made sure Matt had a good understanding of nutrition before he left. Even so, back at home, she was worrying. "You're treated pretty nice in a small town. You go to a bigger place, all of a sudden, especially if you're a good player, people are looking for stuff to knock you down. I worry a lot about that. Because the coach had a feel for the type of person Matt was, he put him in a billet home that was probably more protective than we were. He's a very innocent, old-soul kind of guy, and that doesn't always fly. He's learned a lot; let's put it that way."

Chris says it was her daughter, Jess, who really struggled when Matt left to play junior hockey. "She was devastated. They're siblings, right? They are really important in each other's life." Chris constantly worried that Matt's hockey commitments ate up too much family time, at Jess's expense. "I've asked her lots of times if she is okay. She is rather enjoying that her brother is playing pro hockey and stuff. She's super supportive and always loved watching him play."

While Matt flourished in his first year in junior hockey, Andrew Shaw battled through maybe the worst year of his life. After being drafted, he went to his first training camp, played well, but was cut. His mother, Darlene, almost knew it was coming. "It was hard to get on as a sixteen-year-old, right? Especially if you weren't a superstar." So Andrew turned to a Tier 2 junior league. He tried out and was cut again. Before the season even began, he'd been let go by two teams. "It was a tough year," his mother says.

Darlene watched Andrew become even more determined. "I think from that point on, he was going to prove people wrong about him. And that's what he's always done; he's proved people wrong. You'll never play in the OHL. Watch me. You'll never play in the AHL. Watch me. You'll never play in the NHL. Watch me." He went back to Quinte U18 and played his heart out. "He said, 'I will never play shit hockey again. Never.'"

The following season, Andrew returned to the IceDogs, who by now had relocated from Mississauga to Niagara. While Matt was scoring goals and dazzling in Brampton, Andrew battled for teammates and racked up penalty minutes with Niagara. He was the perfect team player. And there was no one on the ice who worked harder.

Just two years after the OHL draft, Matt and Andrew were eligible for the NHL draft and again had two different experiences. As the draft approached, Matt experienced a setback. He was expected to be a part of Canada's team at the 2009 World Junior Championship, but a month before the tryout camp, he separated his shoulder. After the final cuts, Matt was not on the team. "We respected everyone's decision," his mother says. "We looked at everything. Big picture. And then, from then on, he worked at trying to make something positive out of the year, and he worked himself into being talked about in the top of the draft class."

It was a star-studded draft class in 2009. Matt Duchene was taken third overall by the Colorado Avalanche, then went right to the NHL as an eighteen-year-old.

Andrew Shaw didn't even bother going to the draft, nor did he go the following year. His family knew he wasn't going to be drafted. He remained in junior and played well. In his final season, Andrew was traded to the Owen Sound Attack, a strong team that valued his leadership. His mom says he didn't want to go. "He said, 'I don't have any friends up here. They don't do anything together.' He wanted out. He wanted us to find some way to get him traded back to the mainstream." Darlene encouraged her son to give his new team a chance. "We're not quitters," she told him.

Andrew didn't quit, and it became a magical year. Always a leader, he pulled his team together, driving everyone around in his beat-up old van. It worked. Owen Sound won a league championship and played in the Memorial Cup. With scouts from every NHL team watching, Andrew was the top scorer at the tournament.

That season turned around a hockey career. Andrew Shaw was twenty years old when he became a fifth-round draft selection of the Chicago Blackhawks. His career was moving so quickly, he was still without an agent when he arrived in Chicago the first time he was called up. "He texted and said, 'This is the offer they made me. I know I'm worth more. I'm taking it because I know I could be playing in the NHL if I take this offer.' Three days later, he's playing in the NHL. For him to do that at twenty, those figures that he got? It wasn't great. But it's a lot better money than I'll ever see."

Andrew eventually hired an agent. Five years after playing in his first NHL game, he signed a six-year contract worth $24 million. "I told Andrew, 'This is beyond me.' We have to make sure he's looked after from retirement until he gets an NHL pension."

The gritty, team-first style that got him noticed in the OHL helped him carve out a solid career in the NHL. He had his first fight and first goal in his first NHL game. In his second season with Chicago, he won his first of two Stanley Cups. The team gave each player both championship rings and bracelets. He gave the bracelet to his mother, who was living a year she will never forget.

That fall, Darlene had been diagnosed with breast cancer and had a mastectomy. She was angry, and tired, and frightened. And then the playoffs came along. "I remember going through the Stanley Cup run, something happened, and I got laughing. And I remember thinking, 'This is the first time I've laughed in six months—laughed and meant it.' So for us, it was awesome."

When the Blackhawks won the Stanley Cup that year, a game six win in Boston, Andrew made sure his parents were there. Darlene says they partied all night. "Those days of partying till six in the morning, they're long gone. I don't know how long it's been since I stayed up all night, if I ever did. I don't think you ever could have imagined this."

Andrew's NHL career lasted eight more seasons, but the fights and concussions added up. By the time he was thirty years old, he was done.

Matt Duchene still plays in the NHL. He has scored many goals and dazzled crowds with his quickness and skill. In 2014, he won an Olympic gold medal playing for Team Canada. He's been paid millions—superstar money. His mother says winning a Stanley Cup remains his goal. "He has lofty goals, and when they aren't being met, he turns to God and prays. And I think that's really helped him from getting low, even though when your goals are lofty, you can go through a lot of adversity along the way."

Both mothers believe adversity helped their sons make it to the NHL. Chris Duchene says the setbacks and disappointments have helped Matt grow as a person. "He doesn't take anything for granted. He knows he's been given something pretty special for his life. He tries to give back wherever he can. He tries to be an ambassador for hockey. You never know from day to day—you're one injury away from not being able to play hockey anymore, so you want to make the most of it while you are there and not take it for granted."

CHAPTER 17

Two Generations of Hockey Moms

"I'm proud of what he has overcome. It hasn't come easy. He didn't have driven hockey parents saying, 'Do this, do this.'"
—Jacinta Perrott

HOCKEY MOM JACINTA PERROTT had lived a hard life. She'd never had much money. For most of her adult life, she'd juggled multiple jobs while bringing up two hell-raising boys as a single mom.

In 1986, Jacinta was between jobs and decided to spoil herself. She saw an opportunity to do something she had never done: she was going to take a trip to Vancouver. Her boys were nine and twelve at the time. She bought a tent, loaded up her old Honda, and away they went. "I had this dream to go across Canada. I was raised in poverty, real bad poverty, and had never camped in my life. So I took them out a couple of times with a tent and said, 'Okay, this is how we camp.'"

They drove from Owen Sound, Ontario, all the way to Vancouver to be part of Expo 86. "We were there for three days. Until it closed every day. Watched the fireworks."

And then they packed up and headed home. A nine-thousand-kilometre round trip. They were back in their own beds in eleven days.

Most of their days on the road, it poured rain. They all got cranky in the car. And the camping part was awful. It was Jacinta's first and last trip with her boys. "I said never again was I going to take them anywhere. And I never did."

Still, there were some good moments, including deep conversations with her boys on the long drive. It was on this trip that her younger son, Nathan, daydreamed out loud about how his life would play out. He told his mom he wanted to be a firefighter. He also wanted to some-day work at Bruce Power, the nuclear power plant where she worked. But before all that happened, Nathan told his mom, he was going to play in the NHL.

Jacinta didn't give it much thought, especially the NHL part, because her son was hardly overflowing with talent. "He didn't really start skating until he was five or six. Nobody thought he would do very well, because he was a very rough boy. He had bad eyes, and it made him clumsy. So even with his skating, he was clumsy. So the hockey coaches didn't think he would do very well."

While his brother, Dylan, showed promise, Nathan's ability was less obvious. "I remember it was, 'Oh well, something for him to do.' And something he wanted to do. Really bad. And he always gave one hundred percent."

Hockey is full of helicopter parents who hover over their kids, managing and micromanaging every part of their lives. Jacinta Perrott's parenting strategy, born out of necessity, was pretty much the complete opposite. "Mine were latchkey kids. They looked after themselves. I just paid for whatever I could and hoped they survived. It's an awful thing to say, but that's the way it was. I didn't have a choice."

Teach them how to use a microwave. Make sure they're home at night. And hope. Jacinta worked several jobs at a time to keep the lights on and food on the table, and to keep her boys in hockey. Much of the time, she worked at the Bruce nuclear power plant. When she was laid off in 1985, she scrambled to keep her family going through jobs in restaurants and retail and house cleaning. "They had to come and go and make their own microwave supper. I taught them when they were really young how to heat up spaghetti and stuff like that so they could have a meal and get on to their sports."

When they had games or practices, the boys were on their own to get to the rink. It wasn't unusual to see Nathan walking from one part of Owen Sound to another, carrying his equipment. When he played, he almost always played without a parent watching, because his mother was always working.

While most kids destined for greater things are already playing on competitive travel teams at an early age, Nathan toiled away in house league. And still he dreamed of playing in the NHL. He was nine years old when an idea came to him for a path that could get him there. By now he knew his ability alone wouldn't cut it. So he went to a local boxing club and signed up. He told his mom he was going to be a fighter. "This is my way into the NHL, Mom."

Jacinta said, "Quit doing that. You don't want to go that route." She didn't want him to be a boxer. But Nathan's mind was made up. He was a big, scrappy kid who didn't mind getting physical. And so, while he continued to develop his hockey skills, he also focused on the fighting side of his game.

Nathan could never shake his NHL dreams, Jacinta says. "He had more determination than three kids. I think that's what got him to where he got. He would tell me, 'Why can't they see what I can do? Why can't they see?'"

Eventually, the people scouting hockey games *would* see something in Nathan Perrott. There were still rough edges to his game, but scouts were impressed with his toughness and determination. As a hockey player, he was showing improvement.

When Nathan was fifteen, he landed a spot on the Junior C team in nearby Walkerton. It changed everything. Finally, maybe for the first time in his life, someone in the hockey world believed in him. He made huge strides in his skating while playing in Walkerton. And as a fighter, he was almost impossible to beat, even at fifteen.

Suddenly, Nathan Perrott had a real chance in hockey. His play in Walkerton got the attention of the OHL's Oshawa Generals, who made him a second-round draft pick in 1994. His NHL dream no longer seemed so crazy.

Oshawa picked him up for his toughness, but he ended up scoring thirty goals one season. When the 1995 NHL draft rolled around, Nathan and his mom made the trip to Edmonton to be part of it. Jacinta sat in a rink waiting for her son's name to be called. "The arena empties as people get drafted. And it was hard waiting. Then you go, 'Oh no, he's going to be so disappointed if this doesn't work.'"

The wait may have seemed long, but it wasn't really. Nathan Perrott was drafted in the second round by the powerhouse New Jersey Devils.

His mother says many kids would have quit long before. Nathan never did. "I'm proud of what he has overcome. It hasn't come easy. He didn't have driven hockey parents saying, 'Do this, do this.' And I see so many of the parents now become their managers. They control what goes on in their life. Sometimes I wish I would have been able to control a little more. That's what life is all about. Choices."

Nathan had to wait six long years after being drafted to finally play his first NHL game. It didn't work out in New Jersey, but eventually, the Nashville Predators came calling. He played parts of four NHL seasons, scored a handful of goals, and fought often.

There was never much money for Jacinta to travel to games and watch her son play in the NHL. It was a difficult life. "Nathan even thinks, 'How did I do it? When I had so many obstacles.' And he had a lot of obstacles to overcome. He changed his life around different times. And I think that's something I'm very proud of him for. Even when something negative happens, he's back up there again and going again."

NATHAN PERROTT'S PRO CAREER lasted thirteen seasons, with much of his time spent in the AHL and IHL. He was playing in Cleveland one season when he met and married Kelly Morgan. They had two sons but soon were divorced. "There were a lot of tears," Kelly says. And it was hard. And we tried. I think, at the end of the day, at least we can say we got back together a couple of times because we tried. And we love our kids."

Kelly knew little about hockey when she and Nathan met. Her life as a hockey wife, and later as a hockey mom, gave her a crash course. When her older son, Andrew, said he wanted to follow his dad's footsteps to the NHL, she was all in. "I've always been a little above and beyond. And I know Andrew is very serious. He's a very serious athlete. I knew he could do whatever he set his mind to."

Hockey is a fringe sport in Cleveland. As Andrew's game got better, Kelly and Nathan looked for ways to help him grow his game. Andrew was still in grade school when he joined an elite hockey program in Detroit, three hours from home. He still played football. Kelly worked full-time at a hospital. After work, she picked up Andrew from football practice, drove to Detroit for a game or practice, then returned home. Then headed to work the next morning. Three times a week. "I'd have dinner for him in a cooler. You have dinner on the way to Detroit, then get on the ice. At one point, I had a single mattress in the back of our SUV. Sometimes, during the winter, it was four a.m. coming home. And you get up and you go to school." Kelly and Andrew did this for two years.

Her family helped as much as they could. So did Nathan. He'd returned to southern Ontario after his hockey career ended, landing a job as a firefighter at Bruce Power, just as he'd told his mom he would do. He'd often drive to games in Cleveland, and later Detroit, then head home right after. There were times when he'd go to one of Andrew's hockey tournaments and share a room with Kelly's new husband, Bert.

Nathan also has a third son, Bruce, from another relationship. Bruce lives in London with his mother, and Nathan gets to as many of his games as he can. Kelly says Nathan has been there for his boys; it was important to him because of how seldom his mother was able to attend his own games. "I think not having his parents is definitely a driving force of being on hand for our kids."

For the longest time, Kelly and Nathan's younger son, Kevin, had no interest in organized hockey. He skated and played some pond hockey games, but that was pretty much it. "Kevin was going to have to come to it on his own terms," Kelly says. "Like, he wanted to be a referee. So while Andrew went on the ice in hockey gear, I bought Kevin a referee shirt. And he'd go on during the fun games. And everybody called him 'the Ref.'"

Kevin was twelve years old when he began to take a real interest in following his father and his brother in playing hockey. By that time, Kelly could see herself evolving as a hockey mom. "I didn't know a lot about hockey, and I was like, 'Go, go, go. Skate, skate, skate.' Then I started hearing other parents really yell and pound the glass and yell at the kids. It's like, 'No, I don't think I want to be that loud.'"

Kelly says Nathan more or less reinforced that thinking by setting down some common-sense family guidelines. "Like don't ever talk about the other kids. Ever. Never say, 'What is that kid doing out there?' We wouldn't want it done to us.'" There were times when it *was* done to her—other parents talking about her kids. And she didn't like it. She remembers one time when Andrew slammed into another player and knocked him out cold. "Obviously, he felt bad." Andrew was kicked out of the game. And as he skated off the ice, Kelly watched a parent run down to ice level to scream at her son. "He's swearing. He's calling him a f'ing thug." Kelly was ready to do battle, but she decided to back off. "I'm pretty tough too. I've been in a couple of fights in my life. One of the dads on our team was like, 'Kelly, I'll go down and take care of this.'" And he did, without any big confrontation.

By playing in the hockey hotbed of Detroit, Andrew was drawing attention from scouts. His plan all along had been to play hockey at a US college. He had committed to Miami University in Ohio. Then the 2017 OHL draft came along. Andrew was taken in the second round by the powerful London Knights. And that changed everything. Kelly was still hoping he would play college hockey; Nathan liked the idea of his son playing in the OHL, just as he had done. Andrew chose London.

His mom says Andrew's first year in the OHL was almost textbook good. "He was a big talk. When writers do their prospects for the next year, he was one of their favourite guys. There was a lot of buzz around him."

The next season rolled around. It was a train wreck. Veteran players were brought in, and Andrew hardly played. "I believe there was one period where he got scratched for fifteen games," Kelly says. "That's a lot of hockey. So it kind of went from him being up here to like a nosedive. Super stressful."

Eventually that season, Andrew was traded to Owen Sound, his father's hometown. And now Nathan's mom could go and watch him play. Jacinta Perrott used to cringe when her son fought. But when she watched her grandson play, she says, somehow it was different. "It didn't bother me quite as much, because he fights better than his father did. He's learned some tricks."

The 2019 NHL draft came right after Andrew's disastrous season. "He was actually told, "You're probably not going to get taken. So don't go,'" his mother says. That entire season was crushing. "It was really hard watching him. He just was confused. You know, they're still kids."

But Andrew has never made noises about giving up. In fact, when COVID hit and wiped out an entire season, he and a few other players helped organize the PBHH Invitational Showcase in Erie, Pennsylvania, to give players a chance to perform in front of scouts. It happened in the spring of 2021. More than a hundred players took part, including Andrew and his brother Kevin. As soon as Andrew and his friends hatched the idea, Kelly was on board. "I said, 'Okay, let's start calling rinks and finding ice time. I'm still shocked we were able to pull it off."

Andrew began his final junior season in 2021 and was traded to the Windsor Spitfires in hopes of making a run for the Memorial Cup. Kevin is with the St. Marys Lincolns in the Greater Ontario Junior Hockey League, a team where his father once played and is now an assistant coach.

Kelly is proud of both of her sons. "You know, they kiss and hug me. They still say, 'I love you.' I love it that they still want me around. They still want me to be standing there with my face on the glass, watching."

Two generations of hockey moms. Neither has had it easy. Looking back, Jacinta Perrott says she would do it all over again. "At least they're happy. That's the goal. Making them happy and keeping them out of trouble."

CHAPTER 18

Belonging on Ice

"There are certain things, unless you are a Black person, you'll never under-stand some of those subtle, unconscious biases that happen. People may think they are not judging because of the colour of your skin. But they are."
—Jacqueline Smith

JACQUELINE SMITH MISSED HER son's first time on skates. Her husband, Wayne, was there and gave her the rundown. It was ugly. "He fell. Busted open his chin and went to the hospital for stitches. I freaked out."

At seven years old, Devante Smith-Pelly was already a top youth soccer player in the Toronto region. Jaqueline had bought him a pair of Rollerblades as a birthday gift. He put them on that first day and kept at it well into the night, until he had rollerblading mastered. "And my husband just said, 'You know what, let's put him on the ice.' He loved it. Getting the stitches didn't deter him. He was like 'Get me back out.'"

Plenty of kids Devante's age had already spent years in organized hockey. Devante was eight when he joined his first hockey team, playing house league in Scarborough. "It doesn't matter where you start, it's where you finish," his mother says. "There is this impression that somebody who has been on the ice since they can walk will be more successful than somebody else. But it's different for everybody. There's no book on how to do this."

Though Jacqueline had grown up watching the Oilers in Alberta, she didn't know the details of the game. She and Devante were learning the more complicated rules together. "I had no idea of what was happening. I had no idea of what icing was. I just had no concept. I liked hockey. But I had no idea what they were doing."

By listening to other parents, Jacqueline knew that her son was doing alright that first season. "He was just scoring and scoring. And I overheard a bunch of parents talking about him. "They said it was so unfair he was playing in that league, that he should be playing on a higher team."

Devante's natural ability opened doors in the hockey world when he was noticed by a coach from the illustrious Jr. Canadiens program in the GTHL. When he was sixteen, he went from the Jr. Canadiens to the OHL's Mississauga St. Michael's Majors, playing for a coach he liked and staying with a good billet family. Three years later, he was playing forward with the NHL's Anaheim Ducks.

☙

THROUGHOUT DEVANTE'S HOCKEY JOURNEY—from minor hockey, through the OHL, to the NHL—he was usually the only Black player on his team. "Of course it crossed my mind," Jacqueline says. "It was obvious. So we just ignored it." Race was never an issue for Devante's teammates or other parents. "I loved it. Because we made some really good friends. It was such an enjoyment going to the arena and hanging out with other hockey moms."

On the teams it was fine, but within the game, she says, there are unspoken challenges for players who are not white. "There are certain things, unless you are a Black person, you'll never understand some of those subtle, unconscious biases that happen. People may think they are not judging because of the colour of your skin. But they are. He would be just as good as a white player, yet he wouldn't get the same opportunities. There are times he outshined other players, yet they would get awards or opportunities that he didn't get."

What carried her son were his talent and his drive. Though he started a bit later than some, he soon set his sights on a career in hockey. Jacqueline had no doubt Devante was good, but she knew it would be hard for him to make it. "So many people are telling you that thousands of kids are trying to make it to the NHL. So few ever do. I kind of always had that playing in my head that it might not happen. When he was sixteen years old and going to the OHL, my biggest concern was 'From there, you're going to university, so go get your scholarship.' He was like, 'No, I'm working to go the NHL.' He knew what he wanted to do. And he did it. What can I say?"

By then, Jacqueline had the hang of hockey. "When he was fourteen or fifteen, the game finally clicked." She learned the hockey culture by immersing herself in it. "It's a different life. Learning the routines, whether it's napping before games, what they eat, when to get them to the arena, getting their stuff prepared, making sure they get their schoolwork done. I work a full-time job. I'm a career mom. And I have another son, and I had to take care of his needs too. The breather I got was when he went to the OHL. Then your role changes. You're a cheerleader. You're trying to make sure mentally they're doing okay. You want to make sure that they're putting themselves in the best position to succeed."

THE ENTIRE FAMILY TRAVELLED to Los Angeles in 2010 to be with Devante as he was drafted in the second round by the Anaheim Ducks. "It was amazing," Jacqueline remembers. "We had no expectations, and no idea he would go that high."

One year later, the family was back in California, watching Devante play in the NHL. He was just nineteen years old. "Hearing people cheering for him, it was such a great experience."

He spent parts of four seasons in Anaheim, then played a couple of seasons in Montreal and two more in New Jersey before landing in Washington in 2017. The Capitals were stacked with talent that season but had some stumbles in their playoff run. After five games in the Eastern final, they were on the verge of being upset by the Tampa Bay Lightning. With the season hanging by a thread, Jacqueline called her son. "I was like, 'What are you guys doing? You're letting it slip between your hands.' That's my hockey mom hat. And he was quiet. I had to say 'Are you still there?' And he just said, 'Relax, Mom. We've got this.' And he said it with such calm."

Devante was right. And he played a big role in the Washington Capitals' Stanley Cup win in 2018. He scored seven goals during that playoff run, matching his output the entire season. It wasn't the first time he'd performed well under the pressure of the playoffs—he was also impressive with Anaheim in 2014, leading his team in goals during two playoff rounds. As Jacqueline says, "When you get more ice time, you have more chances to contribute. There is no time for coaches to play head games during the playoffs."

Jacqueline was convinced that her son's NHL career would be cemented by his ability to perform well when the stakes are highest. But somehow it never happened. Twice he played an important role during the playoffs; both times he was sent to the minors the following season. And a mother's heart was broken. "Oh my god, it's so difficult. He's such a good person. And this is where I'm going to get emotional. He wants it so bad. And he's done everything he can to stay. He's proven himself so many times. But every time he proves himself, it's one step forward, ten steps back. He has shown what he can do. The next season, they're doing away with him. It's such a mind game. And I don't know how he gets through this. I know how I feel. And I have to be strong for him and remind him to keep going. He has gone through a lot."

℘

THE QUESTION JACQUELINE KEEPS asking is, why has Devante's road been so difficult? "I have no idea why it's happening. Is it racism? If not, then what is it? It's something. Whether it's unconscious bias, whatever it is, it's hard. I have no answer for it. I don't want to say that's what it is. But it's something."

The NHL has launched campaigns to breathe some diversity into a mostly white sport. But for the most part, Jacqueline says, nothing around the league or in the sport really changes. "Putting out all these messages or celebrating Black History Month, all those little things they're doing, it's just a lot of lip service. It's great. But it's lip service. I'd love to see in the head office. Are there any Black people? Are there any Black head coaches? Black GMs or assistant GMs? There's no way there aren't people out there that are capable of doing that job. But they don't have them. So that's how they make it inclusive."

In the summer of 2022, the San Jose Sharks hired Mike Grier as general manager, making him the first Black GM in the history of the league, but Jacqueline is right in saying that Black players are under-represented in professional hockey. She would love to see diversity in the league accelerated. In 2021, there were fifty-eight players who were Black, Indigenous, or people of colour, and twenty-eight of those players were Black. "And it's not because there is a lack of players. There are players. They're just not getting the opportunity. So I'm sorry, but doing all this Black Lives Matter and Black History Month, that's not going to change things. Have some executives in there. Walk the walk. Don't just talk the talk."

There have been times when Devante has had to deal with overt racism. While he was playing with Washington, the Capitals were in Chicago for a game. It was the trip when the fathers joined the players on the road. Jacqueline was watching from home. Devante was in the penalty box, and one fan took the opportunity to tell him to go back to basketball. The chant "basketball" soon began in the stands. "And he just lost it," his mother remembers. "They kicked the fans out. Usually, he's pretty calm about it. Devo usually says, 'Just ignore it.'"

But sometimes Jacqueline can't ignore it. She sees the game her son loves, and that she has come to love, and wants it to be better. "It's an old boys' club who've been there for years, not wanting anything to change or even understanding the problem. That needs to change. My son is twenty-nine years old. Imagine. He's never had a Black head coach or a Black GM. And there is some Black representation in the NHL head office—for example, Kim Davis, the executive vice president of social impact, growth initiatives, and legislative affairs. However, there is only so much *one* person can do with little support in having Black people in positions to effect change. There are so many Black players who have the experience and knowledge to be in the NHL. They're not being given opportunities."

SINCE HIS LAST NHL game in 2019, Devante Smith-Pelly has experienced a lot. He's played for three different AHL teams. He played in China and Russia for a year. His mother says he remains committed to finding his way back to the NHL. And while he's older now, the emotional load mothers carry never leaves. "His ups and downs, I don't know how he gets through it. I get so emotional talking about it. It's hard to explain just how you feel when you are talking about your child. In the ten years in the league, he's been through so much— many things that we don't know and he isn't ready to share. He has had to endure not making waves, not speaking up for himself for fear of retaliation, making sure he's not saying the wrong thing, trying to be perfect, while focusing on contributing to his team's success and living his dream. It's just different. Devo has made lifelong friendships on the various teams he's played with. What I wish is that when his teammates saw how he was being treated, they would have had the courage to speak up for him when he couldn't speak up for himself. That's the only way change will happen. Everyone is responsible for inciting change."

But Jacqueline has experienced hockey's rewards too, including the friendships forged inside cold hockey rinks. "That's where we spent most of our time, right? When I think about it, some of my friends and family outside the hockey world don't get it. And it's so great to be in an environment where everybody gets it. And we're all supportive of each other. It was a great experience."

She saw her son defy long odds by making it to the NHL. "Every time he has success, I'm so proud, but mostly happy for him. There's nothing better in life than seeing your child living their dream, loving what they do, and watching them succeed."

Other people are happy to see Devante achieve his goals too. Jacqueline's favourite hockey memory is a moment from his greatest success: that Stanley Cup run with Washington. He brought the Cup home to Scarborough that summer. He was taking the Cup to a public event, and it was a miserable day with wind and downpours. Jacqueline's biggest fear was that no one would brave the weather and show up. "We came around a corner, and let me tell you, the number of people who were snaked up the street and around the building was unbelievable. People had on raincoats. They had tents. They brought their babies in carriages. I couldn't believe they actually stood outside for hours in the rain waiting for him to come with the Cup. When I came around the corner and saw them, I cried. Like a baby. It was crazy. But even before that, Devo wanted to bring the Cup to the children's hospital. That shows his heart. We spent a couple of hours with some children who were unable to leave the hospital. Young kids, including babies. He took pictures with the kids, played games with them, and we even gave a couple the opportunity to take a picture with their baby in the Cup. It was quite the day. A day our family will never forget."

The beautiful yet troubled culture of the hockey world—a mother who has seen it all still believes the good in the game makes it all worthwhile. "I've been to some great arenas. I've met some great people. I've had some great experiences. It's a fraternity. Enjoy every moment."

CHAPTER 19

We Don't Do Cowbells Anymore

"Some of my best friends are my hockey moms. Did we drink in a parked minivan in a rink parking lot? Yes, we did. And that was our bonding time and the best time. And we would whine about whatever. And laugh. And giggle. They're my people."
—Michelle Hollett

IT TOOK YEARS FOR the lives of hockey moms Brigitte Goure and Michelle Hollett to finally intersect. It happened in 2021, during that COVID junior hockey tournament organized by Andrew Perrott and his buddies. It's amazing that it took so long, because for years they were living parallel lives, one in southern Ontario, the other in eastern Ontario.

They each gave birth to a son in the summer of 2003. At an early age, their sons found their passion at the hockey rink. Both women came into it with no hockey experience. To say that becoming a hockey mom was life-changing would be an understatement. Hockey became all-consuming. It monopolized their time and drained their bank accounts.

Michelle Hollett already had a two-and-a-half-year-old daughter when her son, Ty, was born in 2003. She hoped skiing would be the winter family sport, or really anything but hockey. "We were never going to be a hockey family. We weren't going to be those crazy people getting up at six o'clock and going to the rink on weekends. It wasn't going to be us."

Ty, she says, had other ideas. "When he was two, he carried around a mini stick all the time, and kept saying, 'Hockey, hockey.'" When he was four, and old enough to play organized hockey, they signed him up. "Now we were a hockey family. It kind of took us for a loop."

By 2014, her marriage was over. Michelle was a single mom living in an Ottawa suburb and working as a dental hygienist, with a daughter in competitive dance and a son becoming a pretty good hockey player. Once you're in the thick of it, there is no backing out. Hockey, dance, and work became her life. "It has been so hard. I haven't taken a vacation. I would always buy my kids' stuff before mine. That's just the way it is. I would do anything for my kids, and I have no regrets."

Meanwhile, in a tiny French-speaking community in southern Ontario called Grande Pointe, Brigitte Goure was living a similar hockey experience. She came from a family of baseball players and fully expected that her two young boys would carry on a family tradition. "I really thought that my kids would go through baseball."

For a while, baseball was in the mix. But from the time he could walk, Brigitte's older son, Deni, was hooked on hockey. "Santa Claus brought him skates when he was two and a half. We put him in ringette when he was three. He didn't understand what ringette was about. It was kind of cute." The ringette was a stopgap until he was old enough for minor hockey. And then Dominic, four years younger, followed the same path as his brother into hockey.

It was clear from an early age that Deni was something special. He could skate circles around most kids, and the only thing that kept him out of competitive hockey early on was his age. He played house league until he was old enough for competitive hockey. And he dominated. "You heard the moms saying, 'Get that kid,'" his mom says. She learned quickly that some hockey parents are vicious. "There were some games I could not go watch. When I knew it was certain teams, I couldn't go because of certain people there and what they would yell at Deni or what they would say."

Brigitte was doing the hockey mom thing while holding down a full-time job teaching grade six at the local French school in Grande Pointe. One year, she was Deni's teacher. She asked her students that age-old question: "What do you want to be when you grow up?" Deni didn't hesitate. He told his mom he wanted to be a hockey player. "I was okay with that," she says. "I never wanted to burst his bubble. I'm not the type where you need that plan B. I'm not sabotaging his plan A until it's no longer there."

As Deni got older, his mother saw that he was good enough to at least have a chance. "When dreams become a reality, as a mom, it gets scary." Deni wanted it. And he had talent. "When it came to tryouts, mothers would say, 'Oh, you never have anything to worry about. Like you would probably never get those butterflies, because Deni's already on the team.'"

It was a different narrative for Dominic. Cuts were always a nervous time. Dominic was good—good enough to make it to AA hockey, where he still plays—but he never stood out like his older brother did. Through it all, the brothers have remained tight. "Dominic's very proud of his brother. He loves to brag about him. They are always there for each other."

IN MANY WAYS, IT is Dominic's hockey experience that Michelle Hollett can relate to, although Deni and her son, Ty, were born just a month apart. Ty was just seven years old when he felt the sting of being cut. Michelle struggled to understand why his A team had let him go. "It kind of came out that 'the Holletts don't volunteer.' The kids who made the A team had the dads that were coaching, who were the door openers, who were the managers. And so my son was cut."

Ty dominated at a lower level after being cut. The following year, Michelle jumped in with both feet. She became both team manager and the head of fundraising. "I was going to make sure my son never missed another opportunity because of something I or his father didn't do."

It worked. Ty was back playing higher-level hockey. Life was good. "I look back now, and it makes me laugh because we were the crazy hockey moms. Oh my god. Like the pompoms and the coloured hair. I would tie streamers to hockey sticks, and the boys would skate through the arch. Like, it was just magical. I loved it."

She would stay up late on Friday nights, painting signs and bedsheets to bring to the rink. She kept it up until Ty began AAA. That's when he laid down the law. "He looked at me and said, 'No more cowbells, Mom. There's no more cowbells in AAA.' I'm like, 'Okay, I got it.'"

Ditch the cowbells. If only everything in the hockey world were that easy.

Ty was ten years old when Michelle and her husband split. Michelle was now a single mom. "Brutal. It has been so hard. We were never not going to eat. I make a decent salary. We went from a very big house to a much smaller house and I call it my mouse house. There have been sacrifices. Absolutely."

Michelle and her ex bought their new homes strategically, choosing neighbouring minor hockey zones to give Ty more options. And when Ty moved to the association closer to his father's home, it got ugly. Going through a divorce was hard enough. Now Michelle and her ex-husband were accused of faking their split in order to advance their son's hockey career. Eventually, the higher-ups in minor hockey called a hearing, and Michelle and her ex had to prove that they were, in fact, no longer a couple. "I prepared for that hearing like it was a court case. The hearing took place just days before the AAA tryouts. I put Ty to bed. And he looked at me and said, 'Mom, do you think I'll get a chance to try out?'"

Ty got his chance after a hearing that lasted just a few minutes. "The president looked at everything and he said, 'Why the hell are we here?'"

That's how the battle ended: the president of a hockey league telling other parents to back off. Ty joined a new team, and life moved on.

"I think all splits are really, really tough on kids. My ex-husband is remarried, and the three of us will sit together, no matter what the kids are doing. So there were days I didn't want to smile at my ex-husband. There were days that I didn't want to sit with his new wife. But I did, so my son would be able to look in the stands and see his family, without seeing Dad over there and Mom over there."

Michelle is still on her own. "And I've always been, for whatever reason, the only single mom on every single hockey team. That's just the way it is." Financially it's difficult. To make out-of-town tournaments affordable, Michelle and Ty often share hotel accommodations with a father and his son from the team. Two families trying to save money. "We just got a two-bedroom suite. It was cheaper. Even though he is married, his wife is fully aware that we are sharing this hotel room. We each had our own bedroom, so it was good, and it's less than paying for a single room. Who's the smart ones, right? I wouldn't encourage all the other moms, because there's a lot of talking going on. Things you had to do, right? I wasn't ever going to miss a tournament. I wasn't ever going to miss a game unless I absolutely had to. So sometimes you just had to do things in order to make it work."

Ty began as a forward, then moved to defence. At one time he told his mother he wanted to be a goaltender. She shot him down. "He said, 'Why are you crushing my dreams?' I said, 'You're eight. You'll make new dreams.'"

Michelle kept volunteering. She never missed a game or a practice. And she was tough on Ty. Financially and emotionally, Michelle was invested in Ty's hockey career. "I thought that every goal that went in was his fault." Sometimes the car rides got ugly. Eventually, she and Ty negotiated a solution. Every time he stepped on the ice, she pulled out her phone and recorded his shifts. When he wanted feedback after the game, she would show him. "And we stopped fighting. He would actually see the video and say, 'You know, that was my fault. I should have done this, or I did this great.' So he learned from watching the phone, and that was the best change in our relationship, with me not criticizing him on the car ride home."

By 2019, BOTH Ty Hollett and Deni Goure were ready for the OHL draft. Deni had established himself as one of the top young prospects in Ontario and was taken tenth overall by the Owen Sound Attack. Ty became a fourth-round pick of the North Bay Battalion.

Deni played in the OHL right away. He wasn't able to dominate as he had done in minor hockey, but he was named his team's top rookie. His future seemed bright.

That same season, Ty played Tier 2 junior and was called up to play six games with his OHL team. The first OHL game he ever played remains one of his mom's favourite hockey memories. "We lost eleven to one. He played twenty-two minutes. I cried that whole time. I kept saying, 'Oh my god, I have to take my phone out; he's on the ice again. I can't believe it.'"

Both players had so much promise. And then COVID hit and the entire 2020–21 season was wiped out. Deni gave some thought to playing in Europe, but in the end, he stayed home, hoping his OHL season would be salvaged. His mom wonders if it was a missed opportunity. "The boys who did go to Europe got looked at." Deni lost the season leading up to his NHL draft year, and scouts had no chance to monitor his progress.

Ty stayed home too. So did his mother, whose dental clinic was shut down because of COVID. "My income dropped down to two thousand dollars a month on CERB [the Canada Emergency Response Benefit]. Still, I went to a fitness store and was first in line to buy gym equipment so Ty could work out at home. When we went to pay, it was seven hundred and fifty dollars, and I thought, 'Well, I guess we don't have to eat this month, but at least you'll be able to work out in your draft year.' All we said was, 'We did everything to prepare you.' And I told him, 'Whatever happens is amazing.'"

For Deni, draft day was anything but amazing. His agent already suspected that he might be passed over. The kid who had starred on almost every team he played for, and who'd always dreamed of an NHL career, spent his draft day golfing. It helped take the sting out of not being picked. "He was okay," Brigette says. "Obviously, he was upset. But he knows he has options."

Ty also spent the draft day golfing, but not as a distraction, his mother says. "There were no expectations on draft day."

Minutes after the draft wrapped up, they were both invited to NHL development camps, Deni in St. Louis and Ty in Ottawa. Both continue to chase their hockey dreams in the OHL.

Michelle Hollett sees only bright possibilities for Ty. "I still joke to him to this day: 'I had enough money to get you drafted in the OHL. That's all the money I had. So the rest is up to you.'"

She became a hockey mom reluctantly, but Michelle says without a doubt it has changed her life. "Some of my best friends are my hockey moms. Did we drink in a parked minivan in a rink parking lot? Yes, we did. And that was our bonding time and the best time. And we would whine about whatever. And laugh. And giggle. They're my people."

CHAPTER 20

You Never Know Who's Watching

"If you are good, they will find you."
—Kim Gabriel

KURTIS GABRIEL, A KID from Newmarket, north of Toronto, was never on hockey's radar. So many kids are always talking about wanting to play in the NHL someday. That was never a dream for Kurtis. His mom, Kim, asks, "Why would it be? I mean, he played AA and A most of the way up until grade five. He had one year at AAA, and then he went back to AA and A. And to be honest, I didn't even really understand what the OHL was at that point. I really didn't know. We really didn't know much at all."

Kim Gabriel's parents were just starting out as a couple when they emigrated from Scotland in 1962. Her dad had been a printer back home. In fact, he'd been printing a calendar with scenes from Canada that spoke to him. He liked what he saw, and he packed up and made the move. It was hard work starting fresh in a new country, but he and his new wife managed to build a life in Canada.

Kim couldn't miss seeing how hard her parents worked, and she followed suit. She ended up as a teacher, got married, and had two sons. Her marriage didn't last. Kurtis was seven when his parents split. His younger brother, Iain, was five. Iain had other interests. For Kurtis, hockey was always a passion, and Kim made it work. "It was still the early days of hockey. We both went to all his games. Even if it wasn't our weekend, the other parent was always at the games."

Kurtis was ten years old before he made his first AAA team. He loved the game and had worked hard to create this opportunity. It had all the signs of being his breakout year. Then, just a few weeks into the season, his father took his own life. He had been the all-in hockey dad. It created a huge void in Kurtis's life.

Kim did her best to hold it together for Kurtis and Iain. "Like, I'm the only parent now. I'm it. I'm mom and dad, everything wrapped into one. The hockey world, there are a lot of hockey moms out there. But I mean, it's still pretty male-dominated. And pretty much all of the people making decisions are coaches. Men."

His dad's death sent Kurtis into a bit of a tailspin. His play reflected that, and Kim struggled with how to deal with it. In the end, she decided Kurtis needed some space. "I think his dad might have been someone who would have spoken to the coach about something. But I just stayed out of all that stuff."

Kurtis ended up back in A and AA after that one season playing top-level minor hockey. But he didn't get too discouraged, and he kept working as hard as he ever had. That work ethic Kim's parents had? Kurtis had it too.

Kim kept encouraging and supporting her children. They had all lived through a terrible family tragedy. Kim made sure they got through it together. "We've always been close. But when something like that happens, it probably makes you even closer."

Even in the back of his mind, Kurtis wasn't thinking about the NHL. His mom says there was nothing about Kurtis to suggest that he would one day be an NHL player. "He wasn't the fastest skater. He wasn't the slickest puckhandler. And if you're not playing AAA, you're not going to the NHL. He was on nobody's radar."

So how did it happen? His mom says it started with his work ethic. While lots of kids work hard, Kurtis seemed to take it to a new level. "Things aren't going well, we would talk about it. We would always come up with a solution. How can I make it better? I mean, it's hard work. But he's happy to do it. We have learned, not just in hockey but in anything, if you want to get better at something, or you want something, you have to put in the work."

Kurtis put in the work at the gym and on the ice. He was a tireless backchecker. When there were puck battles in the corners, he used his size and grit to win them. When there was adversity, he battled even harder. "What always works for him is hard work."

He never expected to be drafted by an OHL team, so when his draft year passed with no takers, there was no real disappointment. The people scouting hockey couldn't seem to see his talent and drive. But his mom could see it. And when some of Kurtis's friends were heading off to try out for a Tier 2 junior team, she gave Kurtis the fifty bucks he needed to give it a shot too. "If you are good, they will find you."

He didn't make that team. But he did get noticed at the tryout. He was told to find a AAA team and come back in a year. He tried out for other junior teams. Eventually, his skill at the tryouts helped him earn a spot on the Markham Waxers U18 AAA team.

Kim had asked her son to trust a system that hadn't shown him much appreciation until now. She had faith. And now Kurtis had faith.

That year of AAA pushed him even more. When his season ended, he took his training to a higher level yet and signed up with BodySmith International, a sports performance training centre north of Toronto. He went for a skate with a Junior C team that summer and caught the eye of a scout from the OHL's Owen Sound Attack. He was offered a spot at their training camp and made the team as a walk-on.

"We thought, gosh, imagine if just someone sees you and you end up playing in the OHL. That's exactly what happened." Kim's dreams had come true.

The first two years of his junior hockey story were far from textbook. By year three, Kurtis knew he was in danger of being cut. So did his mom. "He said to his coach, 'Give me a chance.' He had a great pre-season. And then just played amazingly."

That third OHL season got him noticed. The same NHL teams that had previously shown no interest in Kurtis Gabriel now came calling. Kim, her new husband, and the rest of the family packed up and headed to the NHL draft in New Jersey in 2013. Kurtis became the eighty-first player chosen. He was taken by the Minnesota Wild. It was very noisy, his mom remembers. "Funny thing, we didn't even hear his name called. 'From the Owen Sound Attack.' That's all we heard. We probably heard 'Kur . . .' There was so much noise. But then we knew. It was kind of crazy."

Kim says there were plenty of kids with more talent and a better pedigree who didn't get drafted. Kurtis made it, she believes, through sheer determination. "He sometimes would get upset when he was younger because other kids weren't as invested in it as he was. He liked to practise hard and play hard and kind of have fun but take it seriously."

Kurtis finished playing his overage year of junior and had an outstanding season that helped him land an entry-level contract with Minnesota. He was twenty-two years old when he played his first NHL game in 2015. "Oh my god, I was so nervous," his mother says. She couldn't ask for time off school, so she taught that morning, then caught a flight to Minnesota in the afternoon. "And I'm thinking, 'Geez, I'm going to watch my kid there. He's going to play tonight. And that's kind of cool.'"

Her biggest fear was that Kurtis would make a colossal mistake that would cost his team a goal. But he played well. She worried that he would give or take a big hit and someone would get hurt. That didn't happen either. Her final fear was that Kurtis would get into a fight. And that did happen. Kim's first live NHL fight, and her son was in it. "Terrible. I'm kind of peeking. You don't want to watch, because he might get hurt. But I want to make sure he doesn't get hurt. Everyone else is standing up around you and screaming and cheering. And I think someone around us figured out who we were and said, 'That's your kid out there fighting, right?'"

A proud hockey moment. Hardly the last.

SINCE TURNING PRO, FEW players have been more passionate about social justice issues than Kurtis Gabriel. He has become a champion for the LGBTQ community, for people who have felt the sting of racism, and for those who have battled mental health issues.

He was in the lineup for the New Jersey Devils in 2019 when the players all put rainbow tape on their sticks during warm-ups as a nod to Pride Night. Kurtis was the only member of his team who didn't remove the tape, becoming the first NHL player ever to play a game with Pride Tape on his stick. That night, on national TV, he scored the winning goal against Carey Price and the Montreal Canadiens. People in the gay community reached out to thank him. That experience helped him understand how hockey could be his platform to make a difference. "He has a big heart," Kim says. "When he feels something, he is not afraid to try to help." Deep down, it is just who he is. "Even when he was younger, he would stand up for kids that people were picking on at school. He's very sensitive. Things touch him, touch his heart. He's just a genuinely nice person. He's not Sidney Crosby, who has his place solidified. He's not an established, super-talented player. I admire his courage to say what he believes in."

THERE IS A TATTOO on Kurtis Gabriel's right arm. His mom was with him when he got it after his first year of junior. *Dream. Work Hard. Believe*, it reads. These words, Kim says, have guided her son all his life. "You can't just dream. You have to do something to make it happen. You can't just say, 'Oh, I want to be better.'"

Kurtis has bounced between the NHL and the AHL since turning pro in 2013. He delivers effort and toughness and character to every team he plays on. Every time he steps on the ice, he makes his mother proud. "I think his general manager in Owen Sound said it well. He said he's never had a player whose stats told you so little about who he was and the impact he has."

Kim Gabriel knows that's the secret to Kurtis's success: Dream. Work hard. Believe.

CHAPTER 21

Same Love

"He said, 'How come Caitlin and Erran have two moms?' And I said,
'Because they're lucky.' And he just went, 'Okay,' and walked on.
Two moms. That is lucky. He just never missed a beat."
—Kathy Lee

KATHY LEE AND BRENDA Steiger are reflective now. Their time as hockey moms is over. Their twin daughters played together throughout their hockey career, including at York University. Kathy had played hockey at York a generation before and was thrilled to see her girls play at the same university. Kathy and Brenda loved everything about raising girls and watching them play sports. Hockey has been a constant in Brenda's life for as long as she can remember. "It was what I did with my grandmother. We'd watch hockey games Saturday night."

When Kathy and Brenda look back, their best memories are the car rides. And hearing the national anthem the first time the girls played at

York. Thinking about it still brings tears to Brenda's eyes. Listening to the anthem made everything real: her girls had made it.

And as a lesbian couple who left Toronto to raise their two daughters in small-town eastern Ontario, the two proud hockey moms have had their own impact on the game. "My worst fear was there were gonna be some crazy rednecks driving up our road and harassing us," Brenda says. She couldn't have been more wrong. "I think we've really done our bit to make hockey more diverse. In a small town, it's okay to be a gay family. Just to be gay."

KATHY AND BRENDA WERE in their twenties when they met on a softball field. Right away, there was a spark. They settled into life as parents with their twins, Erran and Caitlin, who were born in 1996. They never made a big deal about being gay, Brenda says, nor did they try to hide it. "I mean, it's pretty obvious. We're just ourselves. And going into an arena or going to a new team, you just walk in, and you be yourself."

Kathy remembers the time the girls were in kindergarten and a young boy approached with a simple question. "He said, 'How come Caitlin and Erran have two moms?' And I said, 'Because they're lucky.' And he just went, 'Okay,' and walked on. Two moms. That is lucky. He just never missed a beat."

As in many small towns across Canada, hockey is a staple during the winter in Madoc, Ontario. Getting the twins into hockey was a no-brainer. Brenda says right from those early days they were good. "There were the two of them, and there was another boy who went on

to play AAA. And you could just see them skating circles around everyone else. You knew there was something there, that they were a little
more talented or just naturally more skilled than other kids their age."

They spent plenty of time playing with the boys over the years. And
if things got rough, they looked out for each other. Kathy remembers
the time Caitlin was being targeted by a player on another team. Erran
was having none of it. "Erran just wiped the kid out. And this was in
the non-checking summer league. The ref, who I knew, comes up and
says, 'I know that was an accident. I know your daughter would never
do that intentionally.' I'm like, 'Oh no, it was no accident.'"

They were, in almost every way, a typical hockey family. Kathy
coached for a bit. Brenda, who had less of a hockey background,
learned about the game along with the girls. And they found a way to
pass on their love of the game to their two daughters.

Brenda is certain she and Kathy were the subject of whispers around
town. "I'm not naive enough to think that people didn't go, 'Holy
cow, there's a gay couple here.'" But no one ever said anything to their
faces. Ever. The other parents simply called them "the moms." And
they were, in so many ways, typical hockey moms. They'd drive their
kids to the rink. They'd cheer the goals and the big saves. They'd hang
out and have a beer with the other parents when the games were over.
"I don't think anybody ever said directly, 'Oh my god, we're hanging
out with the gay people,'" Brenda says. "But yeah, I'm sure they didn't
expect it to happen." Kathy agrees. "I think we have become friends
with people who would never otherwise have become friends with a
lesbian couple."

Kathy says hockey was always a struggle financially because neither of them had high-paying jobs. "People a few times said, 'I don't know how you can afford this.' And I found that hurtful." Decisions were made to make it work. There were never family vacations. When there were out-of-town games, they'd stay with relatives or friends when they could. It was rare for either parent to miss one of these trips, Brenda says. "For us, it was very much a bonding time."

Nor were there gender-defined roles in their parenting. "We do what needs to be done. If the kids need a ride, it's whoever is available. And if the kids need help with homework, it's whoever is there. It's not I do this, and she does this. It's what needs to be done."

In their own way, by living the life of just another hockey family, Kathy and Brenda have helped open eyes and open doors for other non-traditional families in the buttoned-down hockey world. "There aren't a lot of other families like ours," Brenda says. "We definitely came across them over the years, other gay parents. But they were few and far between. And I think we've kind of just done our bit to say, 'Look, we're just like everybody else. We're just hockey parents.'"

They did what so many hockey moms have done: they supported their children and sacrificed to help them make it. Caitlin and Erran Lee each played four full seasons at York University. Caitlin played solid and steady defence. Erran was a power forward. They were both strong and dependable. Now, after graduating with law degrees from the University of Toronto, both are lawyers.

"We told them we don't care how well you do," Kathy says. "But do your best. With everything. Try your best."

Kathy says that's all she and Brenda really did: they tried their best to make their family work. Somehow, they pulled it off for their girls. "They're proud of us."

And they did it in a small town that turned out to be more welcoming than they ever could have imagined. Brenda says, "I put it this way: 'They might be the local queers, but dammit, they're ours. So we'll take care of them.'"

And they did.

CHAPTER 22

Cheaper Than Bail

"I said to my friend, 'We have to get out of here. These guys are maniacs.'
I said, 'Hockey players are crazy people.'"
—Betsy Mikkelson, the night she met her husband

BETSY MIKKELSON'S FIRST IMPRESSION of hockey was anything but good. She lived in Baltimore in 1973. Her cousin took Betsy to a hockey game in Philadelphia to watch the Flyers, who were appropriately nicknamed "the Broad Street Bullies." It was the first time Betsy had ever watched hockey, and there seemed to be nothing but fights. "It was the biggest mess I'd ever seen in my life. I remember watching that game, and there was this pile of sticks and gloves because they would throw them down and start fighting."

As luck would have it, the following night she was introduced to her future husband, Bill Mikkelson. It so happened that Bill was a professional hockey player, a stay-at-home defenceman with the Clippers, the AHL team in Baltimore. Betsy was not impressed. "I said to my friend,

'We have to get out of here. These guys are maniacs.' I said, 'Hockey players are crazy people.'"

Betsy discovered that Bill was a pretty good guy. And eventually, she learned there was plenty more to hockey than what she'd seen in that game in Philadelphia.

Bill played professional hockey for a few more years. He played parts of four NHL seasons, then played his last season of pro hockey in Germany. When his hockey career was over, he and Betsy returned to his roots in western Canada to begin raising a family.

The move to Canada was an eye-opener for Betsy. She'd grown up in the United States, where hockey always took a back seat to sports like football and baseball. "It took me a while to kind of clue in to how central hockey was in Canada."

The game became the driving force in her family. She and Bill settled into the routine of raising three kids, who all took skating lessons almost as soon as they could walk. Jillian, the oldest, played ringette, as did Meaghan, who is twenty-two months younger. Brendan, two years younger than Meaghan, went right into hockey.

It was soon clear that sports would never be the passion for Jillian that they were for Meaghan. Before the family moved from Regina to a suburb of Edmonton, Meaghan was already playing girls' hockey. She fell in love with the game. The move was hard on the kids, who hated the idea of leaving their friends. But Betsy remembers Meaghan coming around: "She flopped down on the sofa and said, 'As long as they have hockey and ringette, I'll go.'"

They settled in St. Albert, a city just northwest of Edmonton. There was ringette in St. Albert, but no girls' hockey. And Meaghan wanted to play hockey. Betsy says her only option was trying out for boys' teams. "We certainly didn't want to be like the family that broke into boys' hockey. We just never wanted it to be that way."

Meaghan was nine years old when she tried out for her first boys' team. It was early in the tryout. All the boys had done their first drill. Betsy remembers Meaghan hanging back to go last. "And when she did her thing, she was a very good skater. It was obvious. There was a woman on the ice with all these little boys. And I remember her just grinning. When push came to shove, she did her thing and did really well."

Meaghan Mikkelson was born in 1985 and was growing up just as women's hockey was taking off. She was seven years old when Manon Rhéaume changed the possibilities by playing in an NHL exhibition game. She was thirteen when women's hockey finally became an Olympic sport. In her own way, she too was a hockey pioneer, becoming one of the first girls in St. Albert to play on a boys' team.

There were some challenges, but Betsy says in the big picture they were insignificant. "There were a couple of incidents with a couple of boys that were dealt with, but for the most part the boys on the team were great, and she became friends with many of them. They are still friends to this day. There was one parent who expressed concern, but again, the parents were very accepting of her. They recognized she was on the team because she earned a spot. St. Albert minor hockey and all of the coaches on her teams treated her no differently than the boys. They were all very good players. From the perspective of a mother with a daughter playing on all-boys teams it is hard to imagine a better experience."

Meaghan Mikkelson wouldn't play for an all-girls team in league play until she was fifteen. "Playing with the boys really helped her. At the time, the competition was better. I don't want to say that the girls' teams weren't good. But there just weren't as many girls who were competitive at that particular time. That was more than twenty years ago. And I think it was good for her to realize that you can play a sport with the boys. It doesn't matter."

Boys' hockey got tougher for Meaghan as she got older and hitting became part of the game. "She loved it. Meaghan could dish it out," her mother says. But the boys could dish it out too. And Meaghan, being the only girl on the ice, sometimes became a target. "If the boys were really big and really good, they'd have enough sense that they didn't need to beat her around. Most of them were good. There were a couple, I think, that went after her. That made me nervous," Betsy says.

There were some trying times as Meaghan got older, including among her own teammates. "They were calling her a few impolite names." Betsy brought it up with the coaches. And she talked to her daughter. "We told her they shouldn't be doing that. And we told her not to make too much of it. You have to go back to sticks and stones and tell them it's just words. I mean, there were times it was hard for her. But she wasn't going to quit."

By now, Betsy loved hockey. When her kids were on the ice, she hardly missed a game. "Watching your kids do anything, you know, they could be playing tiddlywinks, and it's fun." As she watched, she got into it. "I think I was a vocal fan. My husband was the opposite. They said, 'You have to feel his wrists to see if he has a pulse, or put a mirror in front of his face to see if he is breathing.' And I think that was because he understood the game better. He really understood what was going on out there much better than I did. But I cheered."

Betsy was a teacher throughout all of this, staying in the classroom as her kids grew up. At night she made meals and helped her kids with their homework. She volunteered at bingo and shuttled kids to games and practices. She did all the things that mothers just do, she says. "That's the thing with mothers, right? Mothers seem to be in the background."

Jillian played ringette until she was a teenager. She found happiness playing music. Brendan stuck with hockey. He won a Memorial Cup in 2007, then played parts of five seasons in the NHL. He is in his thirties now and still plays professional hockey in Europe.

Meaghan kept improving. It was near the end of her high school years that her mother finally realized she might have a future in hockey. "We were driving to Calgary for something. We checked our phone messages at home, and she had received nine calls from universities. So you begin to think that she should be able to go to university and play." Meaghan ended up playing for four years on a scholarship at the University of Wisconsin.

As a young teenager, Meaghan had watched the 1998 Olympic Games, when women finally got a chance in hockey. Her dreams were set. Twelve years later, she was a member of Canada's Olympic team and won her first of two gold medals. Betsy and Bill were there in

Vancouver to watch. Those Winter Olympics are still among Betsy's favourite hockey memories. "When they came out, you're trying to pick her out of the group. Well, you can't, really, but you try anyway."

The Mikkelsons took in as much as they could in Vancouver. They hung out with other hockey parents, and they were in the stands, crying, as their daughter won gold. Betsy pulled out her cellphone and called her brother in Alabama as the gold medal game ended. She held the phone up and let him listen to a Canadian crowd cheering. A gold medal in hockey. It doesn't get much better. "It was amazing. Nerve-wracking. But absolutely amazing."

Meaghan searched the sea of cheering hockey fans and found her family. They waved to each other. A few hours later, Betsy and Meaghan finally connected. "It was a big hug and a big cry for both of us. Because it was the culmination of a big goal for her. I said, 'You did it, Meggie.' I just remember the crying."

All of a sudden, Meaghan Mikkelson and her teammates were a big deal in Canada. In 2014, she and teammate Natalie Spooner became contestants on *The Amazing Race Canada*, one of the country's most popular reality shows. They competed against ten other teams in a series of challenges carried out in different parts of the country. Betsy says watching the show brought nervousness to a new level for a woman who had been put through the ringer for decades as a hockey mom. "With women's hockey, there is a certain segment of the population that watches it. But *The Amazing Race Canada* was a whole different gambit because so many people watched. Everybody was watching it every week. And they would comment. That was really nerve-wracking."

The show became another proud moment for an already proud hockey mom. Meaghan and Natalie didn't win, but they came close. "She demonstrated lifelong things that you are proud of your kids for. Trying. Doing their best. Accepting a challenge."

If it were possible to do a reset on her hockey journey, Betsy would make only minor adjustments. "I'd say, for me, maybe I cheered a little too much. I think cheer less. Watch more, cheer less."

Through it all, the game has been good to Betsy Mikkelson, first as a hockey wife and later as a hockey mother. The game that once left her cold turned out to be alright. "That old expression 'It's cheaper than bail'? Yeah, it was good for us."

CHAPTER 23

Russian Influence

"The system was so rough, there was no time for emotional drama.
You just buckle up and go."
—Liza Stekolnikova

RAISED IN MOSCOW, LIZA Stekolnikova became a product of a strict sports system. Children were tested at a young age and forced into sports where they might have a future. It was decided she would be a figure skater. At the age of four, her life course was determined. It makes North American hockey moms seem perfectly sane in comparison. "They're looking at a kid's physicality. Are they going to be too tall? Too short? Can they jump? Are they athletic? Are they listening? At this stage, parents have absolutely no rights."

Liza skated with the famed Red Army Sports Club for many years. For a young girl trying to find her way in the world, it was a difficult life. "Coaches are as close to god as you can be. Because whatever coach says, it goes."

Training and school. That was pretty much her life growing up in Moscow. Long, difficult on-ice sessions, brutal off-ice training, and constant pressure to produce results. "The system was so rough, there was no time for emotional drama. You just buckle up and go."

Buckle up and go. That's basically how Liza Stekolnikova has lived her life. She grew taller, was told she would transfer to ice dancing, and then partnered with a skater from Kazakhstan. They competed together in two Olympics, 1994 and 1998, representing Kazakhstan. She also competed in six world championships as an ice dancer. She left those competitions without winning a medal.

Along the way, her coach moved her skaters to Lake Placid, in upstate New York. That's how Liza came to live in North America. She eventually moved to Ottawa, where she fell in love with and married a fellow figure skating coach named Derek Schmidt. When their first son, Roman, was born in 2003, they had absolutely no doubt that he would follow in his mom and dad's footsteps and become a figure skater.

That was the plan.

Roman was two years old when he got his first pair of skates. Liza and Derek took him to Ottawa's Rideau Canal, the longest outdoor rink in the world. Liza says Roman's first performance was for a group of teenage girls. "He kept falling. Dramatically. So they would pick him up. And they were like, 'Oh, he's so cute.' And I could see this huge grin on his face. I couldn't believe at two years old little boys would do this. But he did. So that was his first experience on skates."

Roman was five when he competed in his first figure skating competition. His mom was a former Olympic skater. His dad was a top coach. Liza expected great things from her son. That first competition featured just four young skaters, and Roman finished dead last. Liza was not impressed. "I say, 'Derek, we've got to talk.' I was literally ready to fire my husband as a coach. This was a fiasco." Roman had forgotten his routine. He didn't jump well. And when he tried to spin, his upper body went one way and his legs somehow went in the other direction. Liza was beside herself until Derek offered a harsh assessment. "My husband says, 'Liza, our son is not a figure skater.'"

Roman had always been a big kid. Derek knew he would grow too tall to have a future in figure skating, just as his mom had been too tall to be anything but an ice dancer. That's when Roman piped up with a suggestion that seemed to come out of the blue: he wanted to play hockey. "To me, it was shocking," Liza says. "Because growing up as a figure skater, you would kind of look down on hockey, because it's smelly. They all spit on the benches. And you go on the ice after them, and it's disgusting. You can definitely tell where hockey players were training before, because the whole rink smells. So now my son wants to be a hockey player?"

"Are you sure?" she asked him. Roman was sure. To make matters worse, when her second son, Gabe, was born in 2008, he chose to play hockey too. There was no escaping it. Liza Stekolnikova was now a hockey mom.

It took Roman some time to get the hang of the game and transition from figure skates to hockey skates. He was seven years old before he got onto his first team. "He was a really good skater. But he had no idea of what he was doing," Liza says. At first, Roman's puck-handling skills were like someone trying to handle a live hand grenade. The minute the puck would find his stick, he'd get rid of it. Fast. He got so good at unloading the puck, he almost accidentally became a skilled passer. Mix in his size and his natural skating ability from his figure skating days, and it was soon apparent that Roman Schmidt and hockey were a good fit.

As her son learned the ins and outs of hockey on the fly, so did Liza. Although it was not the sport she would have chosen for her sons, she more than came around. "I think that hockey is a better sport for growing a young person, because there is a bond over team. There is a band of brothers. Sometimes there was some drama on the team. One parent wouldn't like the other parent. But it's still a team, and people working together for a goal. I find figure skating is much more individual. Me versus you. Possibly you can learn from both, of course."

Liza was learning about hockey by hanging around the rinks. "Some moms take the role of back seat, because the father is usually bringing the kid. But my husband was always on the ice, coaching figure skating at the same time as hockey. So it became my job to bring them to the rink. So I think I got more involved in that emotionally. And my husband always had that healthy perspective, looking at it from the outside."

Liza knew skating. The more she watched hockey, the more she could see that many kids had never been taught proper technique. "You know, some people you can see, they skate a little funny, and you don't quite know what it is. We are figure skating coaches, and we can nail it and tell you what needs to be fixed in the stride or the edge or the posture." And so she began mentoring other kids on the finer points of skating. Eventually, she gave up coaching figure skaters and focused only on hockey players. "If you can't skate, you can't play hockey. And even if you are talented and you may get away with simple speed and scoring, it catches up. I actually enjoyed coaching hockey edge work more than I enjoyed teaching figure skating."

Roman's skating was always his strength. It was the rest of his game that needed some work. He took lessons to improve his shot. During the summer, he ran track to help with his quickness. Coaches, scouts—everyone watching—could see he was improving.

Roman was barely in his teens when Liza talked to a general manager from an OHL team who was scouting one of Roman's games. He said Roman had promise. He suggested that, to help Roman reach his potential, the family should leave Ottawa and get him into Toronto's minor hockey program. Liza was sold. Derek hesitated. If Roman was good enough, he told his wife, scouts would find him. Liza knew he was probably right. But the question nagged at her: What if he was wrong? What if Roman didn't make it just because she and Derek were afraid to take a chance? When she was young, she'd been given every opportunity to make it in sports. So why not do the same for her son? "Crazy as we were, we just picked up and went."

Buckle up and go? That's what they did. It was a huge family sacrifice, but looking back, Liza has absolutely no regrets. "I know I've done two hundred percent. There is nothing I could have done more to give my kids opportunities. That's all I live by. If I've done two hundred percent, then it's up to my kids to do their part to take it."

In their new home, Roman played with the Mississauga Rebels U15 AAA team. He then moved on to the Don Mills Flyers and played on one of the greatest U16 teams ever. The Flyers lost just once that season, and it was an overtime loss. Roman was a top defenceman on that team.

Derek had no problem landing a job at a skating club in Toronto. But for Gabe, Roman's younger brother, the transition was more difficult. He ended up as a fifth defenceman on his Toronto team, playing for a coach who was driven by wins. Liza says that year was brutal for Gabe. "The coach would just yank him, grab him by the jersey, and put him at the back of the line when it was his turn to go on the ice. The lucky thing is, because he is my second child, I'm less frantic about him. Maybe he's just less sensitive. I knew he would be okay no matter what. But I'm not going to lie. At one point, I wanted to pound the coach."

Liza held back until she couldn't keep quiet any longer. "I said, 'If you can, with all honesty, guarantee that your method will for sure make my son play in the NHL, by all means, keep him on the bench. Because what you are doing is brutal.'" Eventually, Liza pulled Gabe from that team. He was just nine years old. "He was breaking my kid. I mean, you just don't know what moves these people sometimes. You just don't understand why he would be coaching. I don't know how abuse can be helpful."

Part of Gabe's problem, Liza believes, was the pressure of expectations. "Maybe they look at him like there is more to expect because you've got a brother who is fairly good. He didn't have an easy ride at all."

It would get better down the road for Gabe, as it did for Roman. Roman played two years of solid minor hockey in Toronto. When he was ready to move on to the next level, he had plenty of options. He was drafted by the Kitchener Rangers of the OHL. And because his mother had her US citizenship, Roman was eligible for the elite US development program that has sent countless graduates to the NHL.

Roman chose to play hockey in the United States. Once again, the family was uprooted. Derek remained with his figure skating club in Toronto, while Liza, Roman, and Gabe headed off to Detroit for the US development program. This time, it didn't work out quite as well for Roman.

"Do you want me to tell you the truth?" Liza laughs when she is asked what went wrong.

Roman was big, and the coaches wanted more toughness from him. His ice time was cut back. "The season was extremely tough," Liza says. She encouraged her son to talk to his coaches and find out what he needed to do to improve his game. "Do I think he learned a lot? Absolutely. I think it was more stressful than we ever expected. I think it made him a tougher, meaner athlete. I think this whole experience gives you new tools."

His experience in the US hockey program did nothing to help his NHL draft prospects. Early on, he had been considered a potential first-round draft pick. In the end, the Tampa Bay Lightning took him in the third round of the 2021 draft. "To say we were heartbroken is nonsense," his mother says. "It's not an entitlement. When you look back, you realize how privileged he is to be drafted. And to be drafted by such a good organization. We are grateful that he made it. We are grateful he was drafted."

After the NHL draft, Roman left the US development program to play with the OHL team that drafted him, the Kitchener Rangers. Liza is still in Detroit with Gabe, who now plays for a travelling team based out of Detroit. "This new coach said to me that Gabe is incredible to work with. My jaw dropped. He said he improves every time he sees him. And he hasn't even tapped into his potential. And he basically said when he does, watch out. I hope he has a future. Do I know he has for certain? Nobody knows that."

The commitment that made her a two-time Olympian is a big part of what now defines Liza Stekolnikova as a mother. "My husband is more placid and easygoing. He always kind of goes with the flow. I'm a little bit more of a driving force, I would say. I can be quite fiery."

She believes that watching her kids grow in the game of hockey has changed her. All for the better. "You learn perspective. You learn to enjoy. We learn as much as they do, and maybe even more, because we are actually constantly learning. And if you're open for that, you see that everything is a lesson."

CHAPTER 24

Angels Among Us

"Hockey is not just a game. It's a connection to something higher,
and it's something that lives within some people.
And I can see that in my own child."

—Lisette Kingo

LISETTE KINGO POSTS A video of herself dancing every Thursday. She dances in her hospital room. Usually, she is hooked up to an IV that's feeding her the medication that keeps her alive. She calls them her treatment videos. She does it, she says, to remind others to keep fighting, to keep hoping—to embrace every moment.

A decade ago, when she was forty years old, she was diagnosed with a rare incurable condition called Ehlers-Danlos syndrome. Her immune system is weak. Her arteries are extremely fragile, and she has frequent internal bleeding. She often needs donated blood to stay alive. Doctors told her she would be lucky to survive another summer. "And

I kept on outliving every limit they set on me. Every day is a gift. Both my children see that wholeheartedly."

When she's not dancing, Lisette spends much of her time working on a charity she set up called the Angel Project. It was born out of a chance encounter she had years ago with a young man in a long-term care home who had been in a motorcycle accident. It was close to Christmas, and he had no one in his life. It rocked her. "I think that's every human's fear. To be completely alone." She set up the Angel Project to support people whose lives have left them without the tools to fend for themselves and who have been abandoned by society. Right away, she knew who to turn to for help. Lisette reached out to the hockey community.

Even while dealing with her health issues, Lisette remains a proud and active hockey mom. She took her son, Mikael, to his first skating lessons when he was still a toddler. She says he progressed quickly: "From not being able to stand up on skates to holding a hockey stick by the end of two weeks."

Minor hockey followed, in the southern Ontario community of Burlington. Mikael was a good skater. When he got his shot at playing goaltender, he showed promise. And when he was old enough, his coach, former Canadian Olympian Becky Kellar, suggested to Lisette that he should try out for a competitive team.

Lisette and her husband both grew up in Sweden and met in North America after relocating for university. She came into the hockey world knowing only the basics of the game, and how young players were developed back home. She came to realize that the differences in player development between Canada and Sweden are like night and day. "In Sweden, until you're like twelve or thirteen, if you aren't in net, you are out skating, while in Canada, you have to choose a position at a young age." The Swedish way of grooming hockey players still makes perfect sense to her. "You need to be well-rounded. You need to put kids into the mindset of different positions. So put a defenceman as a forward. Put a forward as a goalie. Play around and make the game fun."

While filling out the paperwork for Mikael's tryout, she discovered that Canada is not Sweden. Mikael was being asked to choose his position. "I thought it was a little ridiculous. He's six years old. I looked at Mikael. It's like flipping a coin." Lisette went to Becky Kellar with her dilemma. "She said, don't be silly. You're putting him in as a goalie."

That's how Mikael became a goaltender. He borrowed equipment. When he tried out for his first competitive team, he still didn't have goalie skates. Other parents noticed. "'Who the F is this kid?'" Lisette remembers one father saying. "'He doesn't even have proper equipment.' I'm like, is this a joke?"

Mikael had a gift for keeping pucks out of the net and made his first competitive team. Lisette watched as her son's love affair with hockey became stronger and stronger. In the early days, there was nothing about hockey that Mikael didn't like. His team would have a six a.m. practice, and there was Mikael at four thirty a.m., hovering over his sleeping mother, wanting to get a start on the day. "And he just stared. And I'm like, 'What are you doing?' And he's like, 'I need to be the first to the rink.'" They'd get there early, the parking lot pitch black. They'd sit. And wait. "He said, 'When I get there early, it's just me and the ice. Nothing else matters. And I get to be in the zone. And block everything else out.'"

As Mikael moved on in minor hockey, his passion for the game was tested many times. One year, the father of his team's other goaltender became an assistant coach, and Mikael's time on the ice began to shrink. "Sometimes he would cry and say, 'Why am I not playing?' They were just kids."

Mikael was thirteen years old when his love of hockey was put to its greatest test. Lisette was in and out of hospital. There were times when it was touch and go whether she could survive her health issues. She summoned the strength to go to one of Mikael's games and was shocked when he was one of the first players to leave the rink. He was usually the last one on the ice. Later that evening, she noticed Mikael was covered with bruises. "And I was so dumb," Lisette says. "Like, 'Oh, do you need a new chest protector?'"

It wasn't the chest protector. Mikael had stood up for a teammate who was being bullied, and the bullies on the team had turned on him. "He just said, 'If you guys want to pick on someone, pick on me.' And he figured he'd been with these guys for so long they weren't going to do anything. Well, sure enough, they did. And he was on the floor in the locker room. He was lying in the fetal position. And they literally beat him."

In hindsight, Lisette is sorry she didn't go to the police. Instead, she called the coach, and a league convener got involved. Lisette says the convener attended Mikael's next practice and witnessed firsthand another player being bullied. Other parents were watching too. "And they were laughing and said, 'Boys will be boys.'"

Lisette threatened to pull Mikael out of hockey when the abuse on his team went unpunished. "I said, 'That's it. We're done.' And he was so upset with me. And I'm like, 'I'm not trying to punish you. I'm trying to make it a better environment.' He still says that was the most traumatic time in his life. He thought hockey was a safe haven.'"

What saved Mikael's career was a call from a goalie scout who wondered if Mikael would be interested in finishing his minor hockey career in Toronto, about an hour from home. He earned a spot playing on a AAA team in the GTHL. And again there were issues with his team in Burlington when Lisette informed the league that Mikael was transferring to Toronto. "They said, 'It doesn't work like that. He lives in Burlington and we kind of own him here.'" Lisette walked away and went to work. "I began taking statements from other parents. I had a lot of media contacts. I wrote down all the dates and times of incidents of abuse. And I basically said, 'My boy loves the ice, and you just need to let him go.' And that was it. He got his release."

Mikael rediscovered his passion playing in the Greater Toronto Hockey League. In 2020, he was drafted by the OHL's Peterborough Petes.

By the time the troubles started for Mikael, Lisette had already kick-started her Angel Project. She's developed friendships with some powerful people in hockey, including Becky Kellar and Hall of Fame forward Doug Gilmour, who are both helping her steer her charity. They raise money through a series of tournaments, the Angel Tournaments, which invite participants to "skate for someone who can't." Perhaps even more important to Lisette, the tournaments raise awareness about her work and the people she helps. She says the hockey community has responded. "It's such a beautiful, strong community. And you see people just rise up and shine and see the privilege they've been given. They've taken that and become ambassadors for us. We have people wanting to start up Angel Tournaments right across Canada."

Mikael has supported his mother's charity, drawing lessons from her along the way. "He wrote me a two-page letter," Lisette says. "It said, 'Dear Mom and Dad, You've given me everything I have ever wanted. All I want to do is give back to another child who can't afford equipment.' Because he remembers what it was like when we couldn't afford equipment."

By the age of fifteen, Mikael had started his own fashion line. Any money he makes goes directly to his own charity. He has already equipped several kids with goalie gear, including a young boy who lost his father in a crash involving a drunk driver. For his work, Mikael was honoured by Hockey Canada in 2020, becoming one of their Hockey Canada Champions.

Lisette gets teary-eyed as she talks about Mikael and his hockey journey. "Hockey is not just a game. It's a connection to something higher, and it's something that lives within some people. And I can see that in my own child. I am proud. But I'm also sad. Had it not been for the adversity he's been through, he wouldn't be who he is today. And I don't know if I would wish that kind of pain on anybody. He's been called home from hockey tournaments to say goodbye to me when I've been on life support. Then he had his team make fun of him. I don't know if I would wish that on anybody." Mikael finished his minor hockey career playing in the GTHL. In 2020, he was a tenth round draft pick of the Peterborough Petes of the OHL. He decided to pass on the Petes and landed a spot on the Georgetown Raiders of the Ontario Junior League. Many of his new teammates have gotten on board Mikael's charity initiatives. In 2022, Mikael was named his league's humanitarian of the year.

She sits in her hospital room, texting with Doug Gilmour, as the two try to navigate an Angel Tournament that may or may not happen because of COVID. The tournaments are important to Lisette. She knows there are people who need her help. And she knows the hockey community will come through for her. "I look forward to it every year because I get to give back. So it's truly a wonderful thing."

Her health issues have only worsened. She had a heart attack a year ago and now has a pacemaker. "I'm in palliative care now. I'm in heart failure. It is what it is."

As she deals with the reality of her health issues, Lisette is focused on what she can do to leave the world a better place. There's her charity. And there's hockey, a game that she and her family love and that she believes needs fixing. That's why she is speaking out so candidly about Mikael's hockey journey and the adversity he has faced: to challenge the status quo. "I asked my son, 'Are you okay with this?' He said, 'Absolutely. It's the truth.' He goes, 'Don't be afraid of the truth, Mom.'"

Lisette is not afraid. "I'm on palliative care. There is nothing that scares me. We are all going to die. We need to die with the truth. So what's the point of anything if we can't try to make each place or each person that we come across a little bit better? What's the point?"

Mikael also reaches out to Doug Gilmour. Lisette says the Hall of Famer is a good sounding board for him. "Doug says, 'I only have one thing to say to you, kiddo. It isn't until you start getting hate that you know you are great. People aren't going to hate on you when you're mediocre or when you're no good. They are going to hate on you when you have something to say and you are great.'"

Through it all, Mikael and Lisette stay focused on giving back to others, and Lisette keeps dancing. It reminds her that even when times are dark, we can make a difference. It reminds her that there is always hope.

CHAPTER 25

Life Can Change on a Dime

"You can complain about hockey and there are issues, but in the long run, these people who you spend all of your weekends and nights and days with, they become your family."
—Debbie Doom

DEBBIE DOOM STARTED A family with her husband, Alex McLellan, in 2004. First Jacob, then Olivia, who came along a year and a half later. It was Debbie who drove the bus when it came to sports. "My husband was not a sporty guy. He was more of a nerd. He would come around. He did become a proud hockey dad."

Jacob played hockey, while Olivia decided on dancing. If you think hockey can be a hit on a family budget, Debbie says it's nothing compared with competitive dance. "Dance is way more expensive. And timewise, dance is just way more intensive. Dance is at least double the cost of hockey. Maybe two and a half times more expensive."

Jacob dove headfirst into hockey. "So we went for our first tryout thinking, 'Yeah, you know, we'll see how it goes.' And he made the team, and the rest is history. You're in it for the long haul until they tell you you're not."

She grew up around rinks, watching her brother play, so she knew the ropes as Jacob settled into the world of minor hockey in Kingston, Ontario. "When it's hockey, it's eat, sleep, hockey."

Jacob McLellan was committed. He watched what he ate. Whenever he could, he worked on his hockey skills. Anything he could do to get better, Jacob did it. Debbie matched her son's commitment, as a hockey volunteer. "Our first year of novice, I had to do some fundraising. So, of course, I take on the role of spearheading it. We broke a lot of our goals. I think we raised fifty-five thousand dollars."

If Jacob had been a star on the team, there likely wouldn't have been a peep of complaint about all the work Debbie was doing. But Jacob wasn't a star. Other parents complained that Debbie was going above and beyond in the hope that it would benefit her son. She heard those whispers. "It's sad. The people who never contribute seem to moan and complain and say that you're doing it for a specific reason. And I am of the belief, if my son is having a great game, play him. And if he's not, put him on the pine. Like, I have no problem. I don't care if I fundraised or I haven't fundraised. You do it because that's your team, and that's what you do. You roll with who is playing well. That's competitive hockey."

Her husband, Alex, avoided conflicts with other parents. He was usually the one taking Olivia to dance, but even when he went to hockey games, he remained detached. "My husband didn't give too many people the time of day at the rink. He just was there to watch the kids and go home and do his thing."

Eventually Debbie found a way to tune out any other negativity. She became an "update mom": while the game was going on, she texted a pretty-much-live play-by-play for any parent who couldn't be at the game but was interested in finding out how it was unfolding. "Very detailed. Every play on the ice. Who has touched the puck. Right down to the second assist on the goals. The hits. Everything." She also took pictures and tried to provide a decent action shot of each player on the team. Debbie had found her niche at the hockey rink.

She and her family had a comfortable life. She could afford to stay at home and make sure meals were made and schedules were kept. The kids were happy, and so was she. And by becoming a hockey mom, she had reconnected with the sport she loved as a kid.

And then her life changed on a dime. In 2018, Alex died.

Debbie and her kids were sent spinning. It all happened so suddenly. That's when the hockey community stepped up. "They were truly amazing," Debbie says. She has trouble holding back tears as she remembers those awful days following her husband's death. The sadness, and all the questions. The bright lights through it all were Olivia's dance community, Jacob's friends, and Debbie's friends, the hockey moms she spent so many hours with at the rink. "Two of Jake's friends, who were playing hockey out of town, were on a bus until one thirty in the morning. Came straight here. Another friend was already here. Two of his best friends literally picked him up and hugged him. Same with parents. You can complain about hockey and there are issues, but in the long run, these people who you spend all of your weekends and nights and days with, they become your family."

Parents brought food and groceries. Jacob's friends stayed for days to comfort him. "His hockey friends will be his friends for life. They're just amazing. Accepted him for everything that we went through and love him no matter what. To me, it's amazing."

Through it all, Jacob hardly missed any games. Same for Olivia with her dance. That was Debbie's plan: to hold on to routine as much as possible while everything else was spinning out of control. There always seemed to be a ride for Jacob to games and practices, allowing Debbie to spend more time with Olivia at dance rehearsals. And it seemed to be working until Jacob came to his mom with a simple, heartbreaking request. "He said, 'Can you miss one of Olivia's dance practices? Because I'm the only one without a parent.'" Debbie can't stop crying as she tells that story.

Since then, she has doubled down to be there for both of them. "I try not to miss anything so they don't ever feel like no one is there to support them."

It has been a difficult time for Debbie. A routine day can go south in a heartbeat when one of them remembers all they have lost. "It's not easy, even when things go well, because they can't celebrate with their dad. You know what? Our days are getting better. I'm crying now because it's an emotional conversation. But things are getting better."

Jacob's OHL draft year brought increased pressure. He was playing AAA in Kingston. Debbie says many moms sat around and wondered if their kid was going to make it. "I would brace them and say, 'You've got to think about this realistically. It can be a goal. But you can't put all your eggs in one basket. Not every kid on this team is going to get drafted.'"

Debbie ended up having to follow her own advice. Jacob's OHL draft day came and went. A few teams called to talk to Jacob, but in the end, there were no takers. "We didn't have our hopes up, by any means. He was disappointed. But he was okay. We were okay."

Jacob now plays Tier 2 junior hockey in the North Bay region for the Powassan Voodoos. Olivia is well into her teens and is focusing on her studies. She dances with a school dance team. Debbie is still doing the mom thing. "Much of what I do still revolves around my kids. I feel like I need to be there every step of the way. Not too close. But not far in case they need me. Still a bit of a helicopter mom after everything we've been through. I just always want to make sure they're okay."

A helicopter mom and proud of it.

CHAPTER 26

Billet Moms

"My job is to provide them comfort, a stable home, good food,
and an ability to just have a conversation. And if they don't want
to talk hockey, that's fine. We always had our meals together.
We don't even have to talk if they're having a bad day."
—Shawleen Robinson

WHEN SHAWLEEN ROBINSON AND her husband, Steven, got married, they discussed having kids. In the end, they agreed: no. They'd both had troubled home lives as kids, and Shawleen says they didn't want to pass that trauma on to other children.

She and Steven loved junior hockey and were part of the game day staff for their local OHL team, the Ottawa 67's. When the team captain had a falling-out with his billet family, the team was in a pinch. Would Shawleen and Steven step up and help? They said yes. In September 2001, future NHL tough guy Zenon Konopka moved in, and Shawleen Robinson became a billet mom. "We welcomed him into our home."

What was sold to them as a one-shot, one-year deal became a two-decade-long odyssey.

Zenon Konopka's father had fled Poland during the Second World War. He'd settled in southern Ontario, worked at the GM plant, and also ran a family farm. When Zenon was thirteen, his father was killed in a farming accident. Zenon nearly abandoned his hockey dreams to take over the farm, but his mother insisted he keep going in hockey.

When he moved in with Shawleen and Steven, Zenon was twenty years old and about to begin his fourth season with the 67's. The Robinsons canvassed relatives and friends for advice, and set off on their new adventure with clear expectations. "One of my big rules is, I don't like to be lied to. And if you respect me and our house, then we will respect you in return," Shawleen says.

If that year had gone poorly, billeting likely *would* have been a one-shot deal. But with Zenon, the Robinsons were hosting a player who was determined to honour his father's memory and his mother's sacrifice by making a career for himself in hockey. What he lacked in natural talent, he made up for with heart and toughness. Shawleen says Zenon was mature beyond his years. In fact, while he was staying with the Robinsons, he bought a restaurant, something his dad had always dreamed of doing.

Shawleen remembers her first year as a billet mom with fondness. And she and Steven watched with pride as Zenon almost willed himself into a solid career that included close to 350 NHL games. "He did a lot of growing up when his father died. He had to become the man of the house. He was really well brought up. Every night he was in bed. Every night but one. He was scolded for that, and it never happened again. He was very mature."

It was the Robinsons' introduction to a system that is an important part of junior hockey across Canada. A family welcomes a young player into their home and becomes their primary caregivers for an entire hockey season. If you're lucky, you might get enough money from the team to cover food costs. Nobody gets rich from being a billet family.

Every hockey season, hundreds of players in dozens of leagues move from their hometowns to play junior hockey. Everything is new and exciting, and often a bit frightening. Providing care and stability for these kids—and they are kids—is a huge responsibility. In many billet families, most of the tough sledding is done by the billet mom. And when it works, when there is chemistry between the family and the player, the experience can be amazing.

DONNA RISHAUG HAD THREE young boys in hockey when her husband, Les, came home to say the local junior team, the Prince George Spruce Kings, needed families to billet players. Les was helping with the team. Would Donna agree to take on a player? She said sure, though she initially had some reservations. "You don't know anything about this kid. You don't know if he's nice and polite or if he's a head case. You just don't know."

Her own boys were seven, nine, and eleven when Sean Crowther showed up from Maple Ridge, in the Vancouver area. Even though Donna was raising three boys, bringing a teenager into the fold was new terrain. "I thought, 'I'm going to treat him like he's one of the family, and we're going to go from there.'"

Donna made sure right from the start that Sean knew he would get good care in her home. "I just instinctively knew that food would be a real thing for any hockey player, right? They want a belly full of good food. I really put a little extra effort into making sure there was enough food, and he liked it."

The initial concerns she had about bringing a hockey player into her home were washed away almost immediately. She enjoyed having Sean around. And perhaps more importantly, her boys enjoyed sharing their home with a hockey player, especially a member of the Spruce Kings, who were the biggest show in town. "Of course the boys looked up to him," Donna says. "They just thought he was a hero. Whenever Sean would go skate with the boys, oh my goodness, they were in heaven. They'd all throw down their gloves. And Sean would teach them how to fight. And it was so great."

Donna had grown up in a family of five girls. Hockey was never her sport. "The only exposure I had to hockey was an annoying sound on the television when my mother was watching." But hockey became part of her married life, especially after her kids were born.

Rick, her oldest, was seven when she and Les signed him up for minor hockey. "And he hated it," Donna says. "'Please don't make me do it.' My heart was breaking for him." They pulled Rick out of hockey, and Les spent a year helping him improve his skating. He went back the following year without complaint. "He just took off," his mother says. "Loved it. He did really well."

By the time Ryan joined in the following year, Donna knew what to expect. Rob started playing minor hockey a few years later. As a hockey mom, Donna was now all in. "Little did I know my entire life would be totally consumed by this sport. I had no idea it could be so all-consuming."

And it really was all in: nights, weekends, savings, all sunk into hockey. "We invested all of our money and most of our time. And we wanted it to be a good experience. So Les and I made a pact that we would try to keep our wits about us and try to do the right thing and try to teach our boys to be responsible for themselves. I think we were reasonable hockey parents. We never yelled and screamed and carried on."

Donna remembers a bank turning her down when she applied for a loan to pay for hockey tournaments. The loan officer said, "Your boys are going to have to quit hockey." They changed banks and got the loan.

All of her boys were good players, and two of them ended up playing junior hockey. "We used to say, if we could take one thing from each of the boys and combine it, we'd have a heck of a hockey player."

They were through and through a hockey family: three boys who loved the game, a father who still played and loved watching his kids play, and a mother who was the glue, providing the support the family needed to keep it all together—all the moving parts, all the expenses. That was the backdrop when Donna agreed to become a billet mom for Sean Crowther.

She now sees it as one of the best decisions she ever made. "We'd go to all of his games. It was a real family thing: we're going to watch Sean play hockey." The first year couldn't have gone any better, because a bond formed between Sean and his new hockey family almost instantly.

Donna kept an eye on Sean's schoolwork. "I used to sit him at the kitchen table to do his homework. He hated that. But he did it." His parents called often to check on their son. "And I'd say, 'Well, Sean is really struggling in math.' They'd say, 'Yeah, he's not a good student. So how was the game?'"

And then, one day—without warning—it was over. "Sean's lost in the playoffs. I remember when we lost, his dad was in town staying with us. Packed his suitcase in the morning, and he's gone." Donna says it felt like losing a member of her own family. "When I went down to his room, I just sat on his bed and cried and cried and cried because I so enjoyed having him there. I used to say to him, 'We're going to make our mistakes with you as a teenager so that when our boys come up, we know what to do.'"

Her boys all did fine. In fact, they added a fourth boy to the mix along the way. Donna's son Ryan had become friends in high school with a kid named Michael who'd had a difficult upbringing. He'd been adopted when he was young, then ended up in foster care. He was a good kid who needed some stability in his life, and Donna and her family provided it. "It was Ryan sort of bringing a lost puppy home," she says. "Mike used to say, 'You guys are like a television family.'" Eventually, Michael moved in with the Rishaugs. Later, he took on the family name, even though no formal adoption ever took place. "He was our son," Donna says. "Regardless of what a piece of paper said."

The Rishaugs had a rare gift: the ability to open their home and hearts to strangers and make it work. Every hockey season, that's what billet families do.

SINCE THAT FIRST YEAR with Zenon Konopka, Shawleen Robinson has opened her home to nearly two dozen junior players. Some, including Travis Konecny and Tyler Toffoli, have built strong careers in the NHL. Robbie Lawrence is now a police officer in northern Ontario. Brett Valiquette is a player agent. Will Colbert works at a family car dealership. The list goes on. Shawleen has been part of all of their lives. "My job is to provide them comfort, a stable home, good food, and an ability to just have a conversation. And if they don't want to talk hockey, that's fine. We always had our meals together. We don't even have to talk if they're having a bad day."

Like Donna Rishaug, Shawleen helps the players get through their homework. "School is important. You've got to get that high school diploma, because hockey is not a life. There are other things in the world."

Without ever having a child of her own, Shawleen found a way to experience the beauty of parenting. "It made me grow into a better person, right? Needed. Wanted. Like a parent would feel when a player tells you, 'Bye, I love you.' Like kids tell their parents they love them. But I never expected someone to say "Nice talking to you. Love you.'"

The Robinsons have been to more weddings than they can count. They've been to NHL drafts. They've formed relationships with some former players that will last a lifetime. "Our bond with Will Colbert is unbelievable. He is in our will. He is part of our executive team to make decisions for my health and Stephen's health. He calls us his second mom and dad. His kids call us their grandparents."

They have been there to see the joy after goals are scored and games are won. And they have watched kids crumble as fathers screamed at them for playing poorly. Shawleen says that part of it can be heartbreaking. "They're living through their kids."

For Donna Rishaug, becoming a billet mom made her own family's experience more rewarding. Her boys have all done well in life, including Michael, who has a career in the RCMP. Two of her sons, Rick and Rob, now run a family vinyl products business. Donna is convinced hockey helped them all. "The boys learned discipline. They learned to overcome adverse situations."

And then there is Ryan, her middle son, who built a career around hockey. He played a season with the Kamloops Blazers of the WHL before back trouble forced him to quit. The knowledge he gained during his playing days helped open doors in broadcasting. For more than two decades, Ryan Rishaug has been a trusted face on TSN. "I just shake my head at his insight," his mother says. "And it comes from being in those dressing rooms and knowing the game so well."

Donna and Les have also stayed connected with Sean Crowther. "Sean is in Vancouver. He lives in a high-rise overlooking False Creek. He's married and works for a roofing company. No children. He never had children," she says with a bit of laughter. "I think that's my fault."

For both Shawleen and Donna, the goal going into it was simple: give back to the game by providing a home for a few cold months to an out-of-town teenager. They could never have imagined how much richer their lives would become as they discovered the joy of being a billet mom.

Donna Rishaug says it's just what you do in hockey: you find a way to give back.

CHAPTER 27

Sledge Hockey Mom

"The sport opened up everything for him. And he took that and went."
—Carol Nicholson

CAROL NICHOLSON REMEMBERS THE night so well. How could she forget? "Well, it wasn't that late when the phone rang."

It was December 18, 1987. The call came in to Carol's home, a farmhouse about half an hour west of Ottawa. She and her husband, Stuart, were already in bed. That night is permanently etched in her mind. "It was a neighbour who called. Todd had been in an accident."

Todd is the second-oldest of Carol's four boys. It was his prom night, and he had just dropped off his date because he had to work the next morning. Just minutes from home, he caught a snow drift and lost control of his car.

Carol remembers, "Stuart hands me the keys and says, 'You're driving. I can't drive.' So I drove." She pulled up to the crash scene, not knowing what to expect. "The ambulance hadn't gotten there yet. We saw the lights of the police car. My sister-in-law was already there. She was a nurse. I got out. I started talking to Todd. She said, 'Keep talking, Carol, because his pulse is coming back.' So I kept talking."

Todd had been tossed from his car. And maybe that was a good thing. Where he'd been sitting, the roof was crushed like a tin can. Had he remained in the vehicle, it's hard to imagine he would have survived. He was taken by ambulance to the nearest hospital, in the town of Arnprior. Carol ran into her family doctor, who was on duty at the hospital that night. "The doctor said, 'It's not one of yours, is it, Carol?' I said, 'Yes, it's Todd.'" She has trouble telling the story without crying.

Todd Nicholson would never walk again. His pelvis was fractured. His back was broken. For a teenager who lived and breathed sports, it was devastating.

Before the crash, the sports seasons were almost the rhythm of life in the Nicholson home. Baseball in the summer, hockey in the winter. Those were the primary sports, but there was also football in the fall and broomball. All of the boys played. Stuart often worked late, so Carol ran the show at home. "My role was to get them there. We'd get in that car and we went. We had a schedule. I enjoyed going to the games. I enjoyed all the people I knew that were there with their kids. Some would just drop their kids off and take off and come back later. I never did that. I wanted to yell at the referees as much as I could."

Hockey was her favourite sport. And if she was at a game, it was hard to miss her. She hollered at referees. She cheered like every game was game seven of the Stanley Cup Final. And she rang her cowbell. In a noisy hockey rink, Carol's cowbell cut through everything.

Her boys were solid athletes, but none seemed destined for greatness. Carol remembers Kevin, her oldest, trying out for a competitive hockey team and packing it in before the tryout was over. "He says, 'Come on, we're going home.' 'What do you mean we're going home?' He says, 'Well, their grandparents are paying for this and that. They're a bunch of snobs, and I don't want to play with them.' So I say, 'Okay, get in the car. We're going home.'"

The Nicholsons were not rich. Theirs was more of a hobby farm, covering two hundred acres. Barley, wheat, hay, a few dozen cows. That was about it. The boys all worked the farm. Stuart had a job in the city. And to help keep the boys in sports, Carol took on a job driving school buses. She did that for sixteen years. Good luck to the kid on the bus who tried to mess with Carol Nicholson. "I remember one guy saying, 'I don't know how you always know it's me, Mrs. Nicholson.' I said, 'I'm going to tell you a secret. See this big mirror at the top? That goes right to the back of the bus. So I can see everything you do.'"

One time she transported her son and his high school football team to a game a few hours away. "They got on the bus. My son looked at me and said, 'Oh no.' He said, 'Everyone just sit down. No talking.'" They travelled in silence to the game. Carol waited on the bus until it ended, not even bothering to watch. "I wasn't a football mom as much as I was a hockey mom."

Like many Canadian kids, Todd dreamed early on of playing in the NHL, even though his family didn't have the money for the skating lessons and hockey camps that have become a key part of hockey development. Nevertheless, he was a steady stay-at-home defenceman who was about to graduate to men's league hockey before his life was turned upside down.

Todd's crash that winter night changed everything. He spent months in hospital, and then many more months in a rehab facility. He has almost no memory of skidding off the road, or of the weeks that followed. Every morning, Carol would show up at the hospital and spend the day with her son. "The first thing I'd do is wash his hair."

It took Todd a long time to realize the damage that had been done to his body. Friends visited and asked him what he was going to do when he got out. He had been working as an apprentice carpenter and told his friends he would go back to carpentry. One day, a doctor showed up and said bluntly, "You realize you're never going to walk again?" Todd was crushed. It was one of the darkest days of his life.

Even after that, Todd tried to wiggle his toes as he sat alone in his hospital bed. There were times he tried so hard, he convinced himself he almost felt movement. He would soon discover that those efforts only provided false hope that life would one day be normal again. It would never be the same.

One time when Carol showed up for her visit, Todd was on the floor. He had fallen out of bed while fussing with the remote control for his television. "He wanted to do things that he couldn't do," she says. "But he had to try it."

When he was down or confused or uncertain about his future, his mother built up his spirits. "I told him one time, 'I don't know what you are going to do or how you are going to do it. But someone will step up to help you.'"

She was right. Someone at the rehab centre introduced Todd to wheelchair sports. Wheelchair basketball came first. It was physical and competitive, and Todd loved it. Then he discovered sledge hockey. It was a game changer.

Sledge hockey is similar to regular hockey, but instead of skates, the players move around on tiny sleds. Steering and balance can be tricky, and initially, Todd had trouble. He knew what he had to do, but his body couldn't do it. He got frustrated and considered quitting. But the people around him wouldn't let him quit, including his mother, Carol, who laughs as she remembers how determined he was to get better in the sport. "Push him? I never had to push him. Maybe lock him in."

Todd had never been an elite athlete before he lost the use of his legs. That changed when he moved into Paralympic sports. He played wheelchair baseball at a provincial level. He competed in skeleton and duathlon and triathlon. He wheeled his way through marathons. But sledge hockey became his sport of choice. Carol watched in awe as her son developed into one of the top players in the world. "He's probably done more things than if the accident didn't happen."

Sledge hockey became the sport that would define him. He found his balance and his confidence, and he soared to heights he could never have imagined. Within a few years of his crash, Todd Nicholson earned a spot on Canada's Paralympic sledge hockey team. He says his mother's voice was always in the back of his head, telling him to never abandon his dreams, and he was surrounded by so many good people, including his mom, who always seemed to know when his spirits were down and he needed a little push and support.

Carol showed up with her cowbell to Todd's first international competition, at a tournament near Ottawa. As she rang her bell, she watched her son play with confidence. She knew then that he would be fine. "The sport opened up everything for him. And he took that and went. There were a lot of people praying for him, I'll tell you that."

TODD COMPETED IN HIS first Paralympic Games in 1994, less than seven years after his crash, and his team took home a bronze medal. Four more Paralympic Games followed, including a silver medal win in 1998 and a gold medal win in 2006. He captained the team for fifteen years. He was Canada's flag bearer in the opening ceremonies in 2006. He won two world championships. He retired in 2010 and is remembered as one of Canada's top Paralympic athletes of all time.

From that terrible crash, his mother says, so much good followed. "It's because of his drive. It's not because of us, I'll tell you."

She and Stuart travelled the world to watch Todd. "My husband will tell you, that old bell gets going. That's when I'm worried." If games became too tight, she often just left her seat. "I couldn't watch. When the chest pains were coming, it was better for me to get out of the stands than watch."

When she did stay to watch, she expected effort. And if the effort wasn't there, watch out. "One time I'd seen enough. So I got down out of the stands and walked down to the bench. And I heard 'Here comes Mrs. Nicholson.' I came down and said, 'What the hell are you doing? Smarten up.' Then I just walked back up." She laughs as she tells that story.

Her favourite memory, without a doubt, is Todd's Paralympic gold medal win in Italy. She and Stuart were there to watch. They waited a long time outside the Canadian dressing room to see Todd. By the time they got in, the party was well under way. "In the middle of the room, they've got beer piled up. Molson Canadian. The boys are walking around with towels on. One says, 'Oh, hello, Mrs. Nicholson.'"

She and Todd hugged and cried as they realized how far he had come and how much his life had changed.

AFTER RETIRING FROM COMPETITION, Todd Nicholson went on to be named Canada's chef de mission for the 2018 Paralympics. He is now chair of Own the Podium, a non-profit set up to help Canadian athletes win more Olympic and Paralympic medals. And he continues to inspire kids everywhere with the story of how, after his crash, sports gave him purpose.

Todd will tell you his drive comes from his parents. His mom will tell you it is all Todd. "He wanted to do something. He did it. You couldn't stop him. I never did. His father didn't either. Sometimes I ask him to do stuff he's not able to do. He'll do it anyway."

Carol Nicholson's health is not good these days. She has complications from type 1 diabetes and mobility issues. Her eyes are failing. But she remains a fixture at rinks around the Ottawa Valley. Carol and her cowbell, and the wisdom she has been dishing out for generations: "We will never be disappointed if you don't win. Just give it your all."

It's advice that has served her own children well, especially Todd. "He's an amazing person. Then, all my boys are. I don't rate them. I love them all."

CHAPTER 28

Hockey Dreams Come True

"I remember the day they announced there would be women's hockey in the Olympics and thinking, 'Oh my gosh, she has a chance to fulfill her dreams.'"
—Anna Weatherston

ANNA D'ARIENZO WAS FIVE years old when she arrived in Canada from Italy. Hers was in many ways a typical new-Canadian story. Her dad moved first, in the mid-1950s. He was hoping for a better future for his family, and he found it in the northern Ontario community of Thunder Bay, where his sister had already settled in search of a reboot on life. Anna's dad worked in bush camps, then later with a pulp and paper company. Finally, Anna's mother got the call telling her to bring the kids to Canada. Anna's home has been Thunder Bay ever since.

Across the road from her childhood home, there was an outdoor hockey rink. That's where Anna learned to skate. She played a bit of hockey there too, and in many ways, it helped her develop a stronger connection with her new country.

Hockey faded from Anna's life as she married David Weatherston, began a career as a teacher, and started raising her three kids. But when Robert, her oldest, was eight years old, he announced that he wanted to be a hockey player. Anna and David were lost. "We had no idea what to do, honestly. There was a lady, another hockey mom, we were friends with. She sort of told me what equipment we needed."

While Anna understood the basics of hockey, she had no idea how to pull it off as a hockey mom. She was about to find out.

Her daughter, Katie, four years younger, followed Robert into hockey. Anna could tell right away there was something special about Katie. "She was just natural. She just put on skates and wouldn't fall. It was unreal."

Katie was five when she first played organized hockey. They'd do some drills, then split the kids up and play the width of the ice. One week, Katie ended up with older kids and played the entire length of the ice. Anna says she did well. "She came off the ice after that game and said, 'I want to play that kind of hockey.'"

There weren't many girls playing hockey back then, so Katie played on boys' teams. And she was always one of the best players. "One father told me, 'You're going to go places with your daughter. She is that good.' At that point, we had no idea. We put them into sports to have fun and some exercise."

Katie had the same natural talent in soccer. Sometimes, Anna says, that talent led to friction. "I remember one year, a lot of the girls were saying 'Don't pass the ball to Katie.' Because she would go down the field and score. She was really upset."

With the players in boys' hockey, the vibe was different. "The boys seemed to accept her because she was good. Tournaments, they did things together. They treated her as just another player."

Parents were another story. Katie was always one of the smaller players on the ice. Anna believes some parents had a hard time watching Katie outplay their sons. "I'd hear some comments directed at my daughter, and my motherly instincts would kick in. I'd say, 'Hey, that's my daughter you're talking about.' I told a few people off." She couldn't help herself. If her daughter was being attacked, she fought back. That's who she is. "I'm more emotional. My husband is more calm. Actually, he'd get mad at me. I should have kept my control more. It's always people on the opposing team. After a while, when she was playing, I'd go sit by myself."

Anna's emotions sometimes got her in trouble. During one game, she shouted at Katie's coach that her line should stay on. The coach heard her and wasn't pleased. "The coach took me aside and told me not to ever tell him what to do ever again. That's what set the tone. I'm not going to talk to the coaches. I'm going to let them coach."

Katie played boys' hockey until she was thirteen. By then, she was also playing on girls' teams, where the players were often new to hockey. "I had a parent come up to me after a game and literally push me." It was a parent from another team. "She said, 'Your daughter doesn't belong here.' We were taken aback, because she is a girl."

Katie wasn't going to back away from girls' hockey—or anything, really. She did it all, without ever taking a break. She went to skating lessons and hockey camps in the summer. She played baseball and soccer and basketball and track. "She excelled in all of them," her mother says. "Many times we were driving from soccer right to hockey. She changed in the car. That's what she wanted, and we supported that."

Anna's two boys, one older and one younger than Katie, had to be ferried around too. And Anna worked full-time as a teacher. Scheduling was a challenge. "I was busy trying to prepare meals and get them to practices. My husband worked out of town a lot. So I depended on the parents of other kids on the team a lot. Parents around the neighbourhood would pick up our kids for practices. And I would do the same if I could."

Katie was growing up just as women's hockey was starting to enter the conversation as an Olympic sport. She was nine years old when a coach made a crass comment: "She's just a girl. She won't go anywhere." Right then, Anna says, Katie's dreams were cemented. There would be Olympic hockey for women, and she would be part of it. "I remember the day they announced there would be women's hockey in the Olympics and thinking, 'Oh my gosh, she has a chance to fulfill her dreams.'"

Soccer remained on the radar. Katie's first national team was Canada's U-19 soccer team. But when she was offered a hockey scholarship at Dartmouth College in New Hampshire, it was time to decide between her two main sports. Katie chose hockey. "Honestly, I feel the soccer skills she acquired are what helped her in hockey," Anna says. "The coach at Dartmouth couldn't believe the way she handled the puck between her skates. That was because of her soccer skills."

Katie was still a fourteen-year-old kid when women's hockey finally arrived in the Olympics. Eight years later, in 2006, she was on Team Canada, playing in her mother's home country and winning Olympic gold.

After she got her medal, and as her team celebrated on the ice, Katie found her mom and dad, who by then were standing along the glass. It is one of Anna's favourite hockey memories. "She reached out with her hand with the gold medal over the glass. And we were able to touch it." As she watched her daughter celebrate, she thought about the young girl in Thunder Bay who put on her brother's equipment and pretended she was a hockey player. "It was kind of cute that she wanted to play. At that point, I said, 'Man, girls in hockey, I didn't think it was possible.'"

The Turin Winter Games ended up being Katie's only Olympic appearance, though she competed in a few more world championships. By the time she was twenty-five, a concussion had ended her career. "You know what?" her mother says. "She still had a fantastic career."

Katie Weatherston spent her life chasing hockey dreams that seemed unrealistic until women's Olympic hockey came along. Her parents helped her make those dreams come true. Anna says, "Encourage your children to do whatever they want to do. If they do run into a stumbling block, encourage them to face the hurdles and work past them. Because we face those hurdles in life anyway. Life isn't going to be easy, no matter what you do."

CHAPTER 29

Hockey in New Zealand

"They'd talk about a slapshot. 'Awesome.
I don't know what a slapshot is. But good stuff.'"
—Tania Pimm

TANIA PIMM'S DAUGHTER WAS around eight years old when she told her mom she was tired of everything about skiing. She wanted to pack it in. Tania gave Tallulah her blessing to put away her skis—if she found a new winter sport. Right away, Tallulah had an answer: hockey.

If they'd been living in Alberta, or Minnesota, or one of the cold European countries, hockey would be a natural choice for a young girl. But Tallulah hatched her idea in New Zealand, where hockey is like an afterthought to an afterthought. Although there are mountains around their home in Queenstown, and skiing is big, there is only one privately owned hockey rink in town for people like Tallulah Bryant who dare to be different.

So hockey it was. Soon Tallulah's two brothers saw the fun she was having, and they too made the switch from skiing to hockey. It all happened without any warning. Just like that, Tania was a hockey mom. She knew plenty about the mainstream sports in New Zealand, like rugby and netball, but hockey was a blank canvas. "I had no idea. Just no idea whatsoever. So I felt really left out as a mom, because the kids were loving it."

She would come to know plenty about hockey: slapshots, offsides, icing, everything. In those early days when her kids were starting out in the game, it had the excitement of an incredible new adventure. "We'd get in the car, and they were just like, 'Oh wow, that was so much fun.' And I'm like, 'I just don't even know what you've been doing.' They'd talk about a slapshot. 'Awesome. I don't know what a slapshot is. But good stuff.'"

Hockey found its way to the fringes in New Zealand decades ago. In the 1940s, farmers in some of the higher, colder altitudes killed time playing hockey on frozen ponds. But only in the last few years has the sport taken off. There are now rinks in almost every city. In a country of five million people, there are now nearly sixty thousand people playing, a number that has doubled in the last decade. A six-team semi-pro league, which is the highest level of hockey in New Zealand, features many Canadian and American players who played some junior or university hockey and decided to continue their careers in New Zealand.

Skating programs, called Kiwi Skate, have been introduced in schools. Kids get on skates by the time they are eight years old,

Tallulah's age when she began playing hockey. Tania says Tallulah and her brothers grasped skating quickly. "I think having a little bit of a ski racing background helped a lot. Their discipline. And I think they understood edging really well."

For Tania, as a hockey mother, the learning curve was slower than she liked. "I sort of bluffed my way through quite a bit. That's when I thought, 'I've just got to get more involved.'" She tried skating, unsuccessfully. "I'm kind of like frozen on the ice. And I don't know what that's about. Why I froze. But I'd love to be better."

To learn more about the game, she volunteered with her local league. While her kids played, she sat in the penalty area and filled in the game sheet. For a new hockey mom who was feeling a bit lost and confused, becoming a scorekeeper at her kids' games was a difference-maker. "I sort of pushed my way in there. Being in the score box was enormous. Because then you start to learn the rules. Then you start to figure out what's happening. And by knowing and watching more and more, everything started to slow down. Because when I first started watching, it was just, like, so fast with the puck. Now I can see it."

Tania found the hockey rink a welcoming environment. "It wasn't so much about elitism. So it was nice. I didn't even know how to put on the gear. So other parents would help and show me."

The hockey club in Queenstown provides free equipment for new players for the first few years, keeping at bay the money woes that are such an issue for so many hockey families. The policy gives kids a chance to see if hockey is their sport without their parents having to make a substantial financial commitment. This helps explain the enormous growth of the game in New Zealand: kids try it, they like it, and they're hooked.

Tania's kids each practised a few nights a week. Because the pool of players was small, weekends involved travel to towns and cities a few hours away to play in mini tournaments. That meant staying in hotels and eating in restaurants. "Hockey is not cheap," Tania has discovered. "It's not far behind ski racing."

All of her kids played on competitive teams. Her boys quickly evolved into pretty good players, but her daughter's game, Tania says, is on another level. In 2020 Tallulah represented New Zealand at the Winter Youth Olympic Games in Switzerland. "I don't know what it is. I don't know how she has done that. I don't know how she has been able to figure out the game so quickly, and how her biomechanics have enabled her to do what she does on the ice. She's not very big. But she is strong. And she just can do stuff. A lot of people go, 'Oh my god. Tallulah!'"

It didn't take Tania long to up her own game in the hockey world. She became part of her league's executive and quickly rose to president. "I can't skate, but I don't have to. Because what we're doing is not about skating."

Tania has set out to make her league a welcoming place for all families. She took a league constitution that was written nearly forty years ago and modernized it to better reflect how the game has changed, especially with the growth in women's hockey. "One of my motivations as president is to ensure we have a safe environment for all genders and ages. We want an environment where there is respect for one another, where there is a sense of community and pride in our club."

The mom who knew nothing about hockey just a few years ago now runs a 250-member hockey league. "I'm not the one calling all the shots. I see my role as steering the boat. We're a collective. Because it's too big for one person to go, 'We're going to do this, we're going to do that.' You just can't."

As club president, Tania wants to recreate the welcoming vibe she felt at the rink when her kids first got involved in hockey. "I want my kids to do the best they can but also to have fun. Put your best foot forward. Be kind to each other. Be that other kid that helps the younger ones. Let's try to win. But understand the concept of winners; for me personally, it's not always about the trophy."

Tania's hockey world is small, and she's quick to admit that. And she has struggled with how to help Tallulah, who seems ready for new challenges. "She has already hit the glass ceiling. And she knows it."

With the help of a scholarship, Tania and her ex-husband sent their daughter to a prestigious hockey academy in Windsor, Ontario. Tallulah was recruited while playing at the Youth Olympics. "With her hockey, she wants to play the best she can. I think she's too afraid to say she wants something bigger in hockey, in case it doesn't happen. Like I say, she has hit the glass ceiling in New Zealand. So it's like, why would you dream any further?"

In New Zealand, Tallulah was a big fish swimming in a small pond. Now she is getting a chance to work on her skating, develop a better shot, and see how she stacks up to other players her age. "She needs to go and figure out where she is. And so far she is doing really well."

For Tania Pimm, so much has happened so quickly. A decade ago, she was just beginning to find her way as a single mom, heading to ski hills with three young kids in tow. Today, she is the president of a hockey club, and her daughter has headed halfway around the world to chase dreams that are so common to kids in countries like Canada.

Tania would love to see hockey flourish in New Zealand, and she thinks it has a chance. "Ice hockey is growing. New Zealand has predominantly been known for rugby. And for females, netball was the other sport. But there's more sort of second-tier sports coming up. So football, ice hockey, cricket even. Ice hockey is getting a real following, which is great."

There was a time when Tania's favourite memories with her kids might have involved skiing. Now, they're all to do with hockey. She lights up when she recalls the first time her children all played on the same team. "And it was all three of them, coming off the ice talking. And I think that probably sounds like such a little thing, but it was really cool." She wanted to snap a picture of them together, enjoying the game they love, but her phone had gone missing. Tania says that's okay. It's one of those wonderful memories that remains captured forever in her heart.

CHAPTER 30

Hockey Mom for Life

"The guys were all in bed by eleven. All the moms were sitting in the bar.
I'll treasure those memories forever."
—Brenda Little

BRENDA LITTLE'S DAYS AS a hands-on hockey mother ended long ago, but when your son plays in the NHL, the worrying part of being a hockey mom never really goes away.

Brenda's two sons, Bryan and Shawn, both played minor hockey. Shawn eventually gave up on the game. He spent some time in the military then worked as a prison guard. He now works for the Ontario Provincial Police. Bryan stuck with hockey, continuing to play professionally well into his thirties.

Bryan Little left his home in Cambridge, Ontario, when he was just fifteen years old to chase his hockey dreams, moving an hour and a half north to Barrie to play junior hockey. He became a star in his four seasons with the Barrie Colts, and he won a gold medal for Canada at the 2007 World Junior Championship.

The Atlanta Thrashers made Bryan their first-round draft pick in 2006. A year later, as a nineteen-year-old, he scored a goal in his first NHL game with the Thrashers. The team moved to Winnipeg in 2011, becoming the Winnipeg Jets, and Bryan made the move with them. He spent his entire NHL career with the same franchise, a rarity these days.

On November 5, 2019, Brenda was suddenly jolted back into hockey mom mode. She and her husband, John, had been glued to their television, watching Bryan and his Jets take on the New Jersey Devils. It was a tie game in the third period, and the Jets were putting pressure on the Devils. One of Bryan's teammates ripped a slapshot from the blue line. The puck missed the target and instead hit Bryan, who was drifting behind the net, full force on the side of his head. The building fell silent.

For a mother watching from home, it was a horrible moment. "You instantly get sick. My husband said, 'I just feel sick to my stomach.' You feel like you are going to pass out."

Any hockey fan who has watched a game on TV knows it can take a long time for information about an injury to be released. Brenda and John watched, waited, and hoped. "When they were younger, you talk to the team manager to get information about what's going on," Brenda says. "Now you call his wife."

Bryan's wife, Brittany, texted quickly, saying, "He feels good. It looks worse than it was." But as the night went on, her optimism faded, and Brenda thought, "It doesn't sound good. Yeah, it just makes you feel sick."

The puck had opened a huge gash on the side of Bryan's head. His eardrum was perforated. He suffered a lingering concussion, a brain bleed, and temporary vision loss. For six weeks after the puck hit his head, he was unable to hold his young daughter. He has been medically unfit to play hockey ever since.

It was a tragically sudden end to a thirteen-year professional hockey career.

BOTH BRYAN AND SHAWN were born in Edmonton and spent a lot of time in their early days skating on outdoor rinks. Brenda and John gave Bryan a hockey stick for balance when he first started skating. "For the first couple of years, he would always need that hockey stick to lean on," his mother remembers.

The family moved to Ontario just as Bryan was starting kindergarten. His mom says it was clear early on that he had talent on the ice. "He caught on pretty quick. He was pretty good."

Brenda was a stay-at-home mom, while John worked in commercial finance. To help bring in a few more bucks to pay for hockey, Brenda started babysitting. "I think I babysat every kid on our street at one time or another. It's an expensive sport. It was tough. Then, when they get older, they want two-and-three-hundred-dollar sticks. But we made it."

John Little often worked late, and Brenda didn't drive, so she leaned on other parents for help. "I was arranging rides for the kids. It was tough at times. But a lot of fun. I miss those days."

Out-of-town tournaments were her favourite, for the camaraderie as much as for the games. "The guys were all in bed by eleven. All the moms were sitting in the bar. I'll treasure those memories forever."

Brenda spent one year as team manager during her sons' minor hockey days. But for the most part, she removed herself from the operational side of minor hockey. She was only there to support her kids. "I wouldn't say too much. Just let him work his way through hockey. He knew if he had a good game or a bad game. Don't pressure them. The next game is what's important."

When Bryan began playing in a junior league as a fourteen-year-old, there were plenty of times when his mother had to bite her lip. "I remember just listening to some parents. 'Hit him.' That's tough. You're playing against nineteen- and twenty-year-olds. I just remember some of the hits were hard to watch."

After he moved on to the NHL, she held her tongue as critics weighed in on Bryan and his teammates after bad games. "These guys are sons. Fathers. It's tough to read some of the comments and hear some of the comments. I remember being in tears a lot. You learn to just stop reading them. Just stay off social media. You know, if he had a good game, I would go on and read all the positives, but a bad game, you just stay away and don't listen."

☙

THESE DAYS, THE CHATTER about Bryan is all positive. His 843 NHL games are the most in his team's history. He is third all-time in Jets goals, assists, and points. In 2020, he became the first player to have his number retired by his junior team, the Barrie Colts. He had a wonderful career.

Many of Brenda's best memories are of the good times with Bryan. A few months after he suffered his devastating injury, the Jets brought all of the mothers on a road trip with the players. Even though Bryan was sidelined, Brenda was included. They travelled to Chicago, to Raleigh, and to Columbus. "It was so much fun. We were treated like royalty. Bryan and I had a lot of one-on-one time. We went to a movie together, just the two of us. I don't even know when we did that the last time. It was great."

The good times are definitely what stand out: the time with her sons, quality time with other parents, those games where her sons did something magical on the ice. Those are the moments Brenda Little treasures. "Hockey has been good for us," she says. "Oh yeah. No regrets."

CHAPTER 31

TikTok Famous

"I'm so happy these videos are bringing out a positive message for other young players that want to advance in hockey. I even saw one of the comments from another player, saying, 'Oh yeah, I played against Washi. He dented my goalie helmet with his shot.'"
—Nicole Ratt

IT STARTED INNOCENTLY. A proud father living in the middle of nowhere in northern Quebec decided to show off his talented hockey-playing nine-year-old son. Andrew Jeannotte posted videos on TikTok of Washiiyeh putting on the kind of display more often seen in an NHL All-Star Skills Competition.

Andrew had no idea that people outside his First Nations community would care to watch his videos. But thousands of people watched. And shared. Then more people watched. And soon, Washiiyeh was everywhere. He became a social media phenomenon. Soon, he and his dad were on the national news. *Hockey Night in Canada* ran the videos during playoff games. While all this was going on, Washiiyeh's mother watched in amazement. "It just totally went viral. We were surprised at how much attention it got."

Never in her wildest dreams did Nicole Ratt imagine that she would all of a sudden be the mother of a social media star. "I guess what everybody loved about it is the fact that he was a nine-year-old kid from a small reserve."

Nicole and her family are members of the Algonquins of Barriere Lake, where most kids get through cold winters by playing hockey. The videos her husband posted show off Washiiyeh's amazing skills, and powwow music provides a powerful soundtrack that proclaims his heritage. "Although we encourage the boys to play hockey, we want them to be proud of where they are from and who they are," Nicole says. "Even though we do get some negative feedback, we do try to promote it."

Hockey has deep roots in Nicole's family. Her father, Severe, spent much of his childhood in a residential school run by the Roman Catholic Church. He was educated in the remote northern town of Amos, Quebec, hundreds of kilometres from home. The schools were crowded and discipline was strict. When he lost hope and felt the pain of being away from home, Nicole says, he turned to hockey and became good at it. "I have this newspaper clipping of my dad. He was invited to play on a junior team. But for my dad, it wasn't for him. He chose family. So he and my mom started a family. And here I am."

Nicole says for her father now, family is everything. "Because he didn't have family with him constantly, he's very close with us. I can see how he wants to be here and there and everywhere, just so he does not miss anything with regard to us growing up."

Nicole is much like her dad when it comes to family and hockey. "I always watched my brothers playing hockey, and I said, 'I want to play.' So my dad put me on his team that he was coaching, and from U15 to U16, I played on a boys' hockey team." She was a goalie, and she stuck with it well into her adult life, as her kids were growing up. "I tried my best. I love the sport."

Washiiyeh watched his mom and decided he would be a goalie too, but before long, he switched to playing defence. "He was very good in net. But what attracted him to playing out of the net was seeing all his friends scoring. And once he saw that, he left the pads and went as a player."

Two of Nicole's sons play hockey. She and her family spend many hours each week in hockey rinks, and even more time in the car. The nearest indoor rink is an hour and a half south of their home. "It's a blink for us because we're used to it. It's what we've always done. For everything. We've had to always travel to town." She wouldn't even call it a sacrifice. It's just what Nicole does for family and for hockey, her two loves in life.

There are times she does not feel love coming back. Just like her father, she knows about racism. "There are times I go sit down at the rink. Parents would see me. And they would start moving away a bit. Pretty soon, there is a huge gap between me and the other parents and I'm sitting alone."

Still there have been victories for Nicole and her family. Her husband, Andrew, has become the first Indigenous person to run the minor hockey league in their region. "When Indigenous players saw a Native person become the president, it was a big plus for us. They felt like it was something that could help them have the same opportunities as the rest of the players."

Opportunities. That's what Nicole feels hockey provides her family and her community. She is the director of the Kitiganik Health and Wellness Centre, and she regularly tries to help young people who've lost hope. She has seen far too many kids from her community take their own lives. Hockey gives her hope because kids are reminded that they have support. "Everybody goes to watch. We have uncles, aunts, and we have parents. My father hardly misses a game. We're such a big hockey family."

Nicole's family now spends even more time travelling to and from hockey rinks. Washiiyeh plays competitive hockey, with many of his games being played just outside Ottawa, three and a half hours from home. Because of the videos, it is not unusual for Washiiyeh to be recognized at hockey rinks.

Her sons also understand that racism is a sad reality at the hockey rink. "We hear the occasional name calling for Wash. So he has to work twice as hard on a team in order to maintain his spot. We try to show people that he's our son. He's no different than your kid. We just keep telling Wash, 'Show them how you can play, regardless of your background. Show them.'" But even though he's nine years old, people don't care. "My husband was saying, 'How are we going to make them see him as a player and not as the only Native kid on the team?' I wish I had an easy answer for that."

That's why Washiiyeh and his father continue making the videos and why Nicole continues to encourage them. She wants people to see her son for what he is: a talented, passionate young hockey player. "I'm so happy these videos are bringing out a positive message for other young players that want to advance in hockey. I even saw one of the comments from another player saying 'Oh yeah, I played against Washi. He dented my goalie helmet with his shot.'"

CHAPTER 32

Lifesaver

"They talk a lot about being able to get along with other kids, no matter what the behaviours of kids are on the team. They don't really take it personally. They realize we all come with baggage."
—Bonnie O'Reilly

You learn plenty of important life lessons growing up in a big family. And Bonnie O'Reilly's family was big. She was one of fourteen kids living under the same roof in the east end of Toronto. "My husband uses a saying with us, whenever I get really upset with him, 'There were too many rats in the cage growing up.'"

Fourteen kids. Bonnie says it was kind of crazy. And it probably was. To make it work, Bonnie and her siblings pitched in and helped each other. There was a spirit of generosity and co-operation that kept all the moving parts together. They helped each other with homework. They played sports together, including hockey. And they competed.

With so many kids, how could even simple things not evolve into a competition?

Bonnie carried those life lessons with her as she began raising her own family, two boys and two girls. All of them became hockey players. Bonnie's family unit when she was growing up had been tight-knit and supportive. She made sure her own family was like that too. And when she missed the energy and the chaos of a big family, she found a solution.

Bonnie and her husband, Brian, were both social workers, raising their family in Seaforth, Ontario, a tiny community about an hour north of London. In 1991, when Bonnie was pregnant with her third child, Ryan, she and Brian took over a group home for vulnerable youth. Her whole family moved in, and it became their home too. Over the years, Bonnie and Brian became foster parents to forty-seven teenagers. Those life lessons Bonnie learned growing up in a big family? Now the four O'Reilly kids were learning them too.

Much of the time, there were four foster kids living with the O'Reillys. Some stayed for just a few weeks; others were there for years. Bonnie says you can only imagine the challenges. "We definitely got kids who were having some difficulty in their lives, and it came with some challenging behaviour."

Being part of a foster home became the norm for Bonnie's own kids. From the day Ryan came home from the hospital, it was all he knew. "When I hear them speak about it, they all feel that it was beneficial to them in their lives to be aware that not everybody has it good."

The O'Reilly kids had an older cousin who played in the OHL with the Windsor Spitfires, and Bonnie says that helped her boys see the possibilities that existed in hockey. "It was like, 'I'm going to the NHL.' You never think they really are. But lots of kids have the dream."

Cal and Ryan O'Reilly dreamed big, and they had the talent and drive to back up their dreams. And plenty of people in their small town were more than happy to help them improve. When the boys wondered if they could get in some practice before school or at lunchtime at the local skating rink, Brian put in a call to Graham Nesbitt, who was running the rink, to ask if it was possible. Bonnie says Graham made it happen. "It wasn't like, 'Oh, they're going to the NHL, I'm going to let them on the ice.' It was nothing like that. It was just, 'They're really driven. They want to skate. I'm going to let them.'"

Brian was a minor hockey coach. Often, when Graham opened the rink in off-hours, Brian joined Cal and Ryan and any other local kids who wanted to improve. Bonnie never forgot Graham's selfless kindness. "Graham was great with a lot of kids. Very nice of him to do that."

Bonnie had the foster kids, and she had her own kids, who were all good hockey players and played non-stop. Her life was busy. "I kind of recreated the crazy lifestyle I grew up in."

The foster kids provided special challenges for Bonnie. She remembers one particularly difficult night when her own kids were being run to hockey rinks. She stayed behind because it was supposed to be a special night for one of her foster kids. "And his mom was supposed to come and take him to McDonald's. Well, she called and cancelled. So he's watching us going to the ends of the earth for a hockey game and standing there going, 'What's wrong with me?' And I tried to make that night special. Our kids could see that, and see the pain of that child being let down. And I'm not trying to beat down the parent, because the poor mother has her own challenges and struggles to deal with. But when you have the child with you, and their heart gets broken, it's hard. It's sad."

There were victories along the way, reminding Bonnie that there was hope. But often, she says, they were small victories. "To me, if a kid is not getting suspended, if a kid is not getting any criminal charges, that's kind of a victory. So if a placement is lasting and they're willing to stay with you, that's a success."

The O'Reilly kids saw all this and learned from it, Bonnie says. "They talk a lot about being able to get along with other kids, no matter what the behaviours of kids are on the team. They don't really take it personally. They realize we all come with baggage."

Sports became a bonding ground in the O'Reilly home. They had a basketball net and a volleyball court set up in the summer, a hockey rink in the winter. The O'Reilly kids played alongside the foster kids. It's what families do. And that's what Bonnie and Brian were trying to build: one big family. There were plenty of times when life got complicated, but Bonnie says her own kids never allowed their focus on hockey to waver. Her two boys, in particular, did all they could to make it to the NHL. "They set aside the partying piece. They kind of stepped away a bit from choosing to do that and socializing. They chose instead to get up at six and train and work out. There's lots of talented kids. But if you don't do that legwork and keep pushing and pushing, you're not necessarily going to arrive and stay in professional hockey."

Both boys made it. Cal, who is five years older, made the jump first. Two years after joining the Windsor Spitfires, he was drafted by the Nashville Predators in 2005. He was twenty-two years old when he played in his first NHL game in 2008.

Everything happened a bit faster for Ryan. He was the first overall draft pick by the OHL's Erie Otters in 2007. Two years later, still just eighteen years old, he was playing in the NHL with the Colorado Avalanche, who drafted him in the second round in 2009. It was a surprise to many people, including Bonnie, that no team took him in the first round. "So all that anxiety. 'Are they going to call my name?' At the end, he just turned to me and said, 'I'm going to be sick.' And we kind of all felt that way. It was all really draining. And then he went early the next day. It was wonderful."

It has been close to two decades since Cal was drafted. He played with five different NHL teams, but his biggest success has come in the AHL. He is now among the league's all-time leaders in games played and scoring. And he's still going strong.

Ryan has become a star in the NHL. He was the St. Louis Blues' best player in 2019, the year they won the Stanley Cup. It was an emotional time for Bonnie when Ryan brought the Cup home that summer so his community could celebrate with him. "I was really proud of him that he was willing to do that and give back, because so many people loved it and wanted to just be part of it. And he allowed it to happen."

છ

WHILE THE PEOPLE OF Seaforth were celebrating with Ryan, one of his early supporters, Graham Nesbitt, was battling a kidney disorder. He had been diagnosed in 2011, and his health was getting worse. He needed a new kidney. When he reached out to Bonnie to ask if her boys could use their social media platforms to help him find a lifesaving donor, it got Bonnie thinking. "I said to Brian, he was so good to our kids, I'm going to check it out."

Bonnie was a perfect match. In 2021, she donated a kidney to the man who had done so much to help her boys make it. "He was pretty choked up. It was pretty awesome."

It's what they do in small towns: they find ways to help each other without expecting anything back. Bonnie O'Reilly donated her kidney so a neighbour could stay alive. "Everything was perfect. So I'm really glad. He's a good guy."

BONNIE AND BRIAN'S TWO daughters also played high-level hockey. Tara, who was born between Cal and Ryan, studied in Ottawa and captained the Carleton University women's team. Shannon, the youngest, played junior hockey close to home. All of her kids, Bonnie says, made it on their own. "We would never push them. Never. As social workers, we definitely believe we don't know what's best for our kids and never have. They were pretty self-driven. Never did we say 'Oh, you should train.' 'You should take a break' is more what we might say."

It has been hit-and-miss with the foster kids who passed through their lives. Some have stayed in touch over the years simply to say thank you. "It's not like we were looking for gratitude," Bonnie says. "But it was nice to hear later that they appreciate it and that they're saying 'Sorry I was such a such-and-such to you guys.' It's okay. We understood their anger was justified given their lives, and we tried not to take it personally if it was ever dished our way."

Their complicated home life provided plenty of lessons for Bonnie's kids. And now that they are adults, she is learning from them. "They have achieved far higher than I ever have. If you work hard enough and overcome obstacles along the way, you absolutely can reach your dreams. They've shown us that."

CHAPTER 33

Fight for Your Right

"I think the biggest difference I've made is maybe to open one or two eyes to the capabilities that are beyond the people who get the big contracts at the NHL level. There is a love for the sport at the grassroots level."
—Jen O'Brien

PARENTS AREN'T GIVEN A road map to help them raise children, leaving most parents to wing it. And there is certainly no road map for parents of children with special needs. Jen O'Brien's two daughters both have a mild form of cerebral palsy, and she has been forced to create her own road map. What guides her is a simple belief that all kids want to be included and given a chance to shine. Ever since her daughters were born, she has been knocking down barriers to create opportunities for kids who weren't being given their chance. Hockey has provided her with a platform to help her own kids and so many others.

Her passion for helping is rooted in her own upbringing. Her mom had disabilities, and Jen learned first-hand how complicated life can be when disability is part of it. "She had more than twenty back surgeries when I was growing up, and she was always in the hospital, and so I was kind of raised by a band of people. I had a whole tribe." She hopes to have the same sort of impact on others that her tribe had on her.

Her life as a child built the foundation for who she would be as a mother, and later as an advocate. When Paige was four and Maggie two, she set out to help them get better control of their body movements and see the world of possibilities that lay before them. She showed them the beauty they could create through movement. She and her daughters created works of art together. They didn't use paintbrushes; they used their whole bodies to paint. The messier the better. Something just clicked. During that painting session with her daughters, she sensed a real opportunity to help others with special needs. She launched the Magic Paintbrush Project, holding painting sessions where she lived in Binghamton, New York. People with disabilities came out and discovered what Jen's daughters had learned: they were capable of creating beautiful artworks. They were shown a world of possibilities where once there were only limitations. Paint and canvas became a perfect way to capture a special memory.

The Magic Paintbrush Project started out small, but it grew. Thousands of people have been part of its workshops over the past two decades, experiencing the possibilities for people with disabilities. Initially, Jen gave away the artwork they were creating, but then people started offering money and her program grew even bigger. She had money to fund more workshops. And when community leaders began coming out to paint, she had a profile.

And that's where hockey comes into the picture. Among those who got on board were the Binghamton Senators, the farm team for the Ottawa Senators at the time. It was magic. The players mucked around in the paint with the kids in the program. They drew portraits and silly faces, and they laughed and bonded. Year after year, they would get together and do it again. It became a highlight of the year for the players. And for Jen O'Brien, it was an eye-opener. Hockey hadn't previously been part of her life, but now she was seeing it at its best.

After that, she jumped with both feet into learning more about hockey. She loved everything about the players and their energy and commitment to her cause. With the game of hockey, she could see amazing possibilities to help families of children with special needs.

Jen O'Brien is now the executive director of the American Special Hockey Association (ASHA). There are more than a hundred teams from across the United States under the umbrella of the organization. People who were told all their lives that they were not capable of playing now can be part of a team. They put on skates. Sometimes they fall, but they get back up, always with the joy of doing something new and exciting. Jen says, "I love rules, because rules tell me all the things I can't do. They don't tell me all the things I *can* do. I coined the phrase 'tools, materials, and opportunity.' So my role is to put the tools, materials, and opportunity in front of somebody and then allow them to be who they are."

Her daughters are in their twenties now. Although they have never played hockey, they are involved with the ASHA as volunteers. Jen has watched their confidence grow the more time they spend in a hockey rink. And they have, in so many ways, inspired their mother to go out and make a difference through the sport.

The Binghamton Senators left town a few years ago. The Binghamton Black Bears of the Federal Prospects Hockey League have filled the city's hockey void and continue to champion Jen's work. Several NHL teams are now on board. Through her hockey contacts, Jen is now a member of the NHL's Youth Hockey Inclusion Committee. Her focus is helping make hockey more accessible for people with disabilities.

In 2017, Jen O'Brien was named a New York State Woman of Distinction, and in 2018, she was chosen as her state's Mother of the Year. She is now a delegate to the UN's Commission on the Status of Women. "I think the biggest difference I've made is maybe to open one or two eyes to the capabilities that are beyond the people who get the big contracts at the NHL level. There is a love for the sport at the grassroots level. I hope I've started some conversations. I hope I've pissed people off enough that maybe they're starting to see things they didn't see before. I think if there is one big difference, there's this group of people that are now playing hockey, and using their opportunities, where before they were not welcomed and couldn't play."

Jen has never considered herself a hockey mom, even though she has done what so many hockey moms do: she has pushed and advocated and kicked down doors to make hockey more inclusive. "You have to be fearless in this. They always say moms don't have a manual. It's messy. It can get ugly. You occasionally get shit on. All those things that are messy about being a mom—finding solutions on the fly, doing all the planning, and all those things that we do naturally, instinctively—really hold it all together."

There are plenty of players with special needs who will tell you that, in so many ways, Jen O'Brien is the perfect hockey mom. She has provided so many with the tools, materials and opportunity to play.

CHAPTER 34

An Unexpected Journey

*"To see your kid out there playing Canada's game, to have
that experience and feel the joy it has brought to so many
families and to our family, it's just incredible."*
—Sandra Wallace

IT IS SAFE TO say Sandra Wallace never expected that she would one day be sitting in a rink and watching her daughter Camryn playing hockey. "Not part of the plan." Even before Camryn was born in 2005, there were signs that things just weren't right. Four months into the pregnancy, doctors discovered a heart defect. Sandra and her husband, Ross, were told it could be a sign of other serious problems. There was still a chance to do more tests and possibly terminate the pregnancy. Sandra and Ross said no. "We're going to play the hand we were dealt" was her answer.

Camryn was considered a high-risk pregnancy because of the heart defect, and when she was born, doctors scooped her up and brought her for tests right away. Less than a half-hour later, they returned Camryn to Sandra, and a doctor leaned in and quietly broke the news: Camryn had Down syndrome. "And we were like, 'Okay.' That shock that hits you."

Down syndrome is a genetic disorder that causes developmental delays. These days, more and more babies born with Down syndrome go on to live healthy and fulfilling lives. But hearing that news minutes after giving birth . . . Sandra says, "It is like a Mack truck hit you."

Sandra's mother was with her in the hospital. "I was holding on to the baby, and then they took her away, and my mom was like, 'Sandra, it's going to be fine. She's going to do everything that everyone else is going to do. She's just going to be fine. Wait and see.'"

A SIMILAR STORY HAD played out for Linda Lefebvre a few years earlier when her son Tysen was being delivered. "Right away, his skull and eyes were bulged out. We knew something was wrong."

Tysen was born with a rare genetic disorder called Pfeiffer syndrome type II, which causes some skull bones to fuse too soon. His skull is in a cloverleaf shape, creating breathing and eating issues. Within weeks of being born, Tysen was undergoing the first of dozens of operations he'd have to endure. Because of his illness, his elbows are fused together. Mobility is an issue because of tightness in his knees and ankles.

One doctor told Linda and her husband, Scott, that Tysen might never walk or talk. Another offered more optimism, telling Linda he would be just fine. "He was right," she says.

ひ

FOR BOTH MOTHERS, THE learning curve that followed was steep. They were raising children with severe health issues—children who would in no way be leading so-called normal lives. Right away, Sandra and Linda knew their lives were changing too. They were being thrown into a great unknown.

While the two mothers knew the journey would come with great challenges, they never expected there to be so many rewards. Camryn and Tysen have both developed into remarkable people. Camryn has an energy that lights up a room. Sandra says it's impossible to imagine what life would be like without her. "She has brought so many amazing opportunities and experiences to our family. It's pretty incredible." It is the same with Tysen. Linda says he has faced obstacles his whole life and has never voiced a word of complaint. "Yes, we went through some difficult times and lots of stress and heartache, but he's always brought us so much joy that it hasn't been a struggle by any means."

Eventually, these two moms would be brought together through the game of hockey. They would spend countless hours together, sitting in cold rinks, watching their children out on the ice. Never in a million years would either have thought it possible.

SANDRA AND ROSS WALLACE set out to learn everything they could about Down syndrome. They wanted to know the challenges they would face. More importantly, they were searching for opportunities to enrich Camryn's life. That's when hockey came into the conversation.

Ross knew almost nothing about the sport. He'd grown up in New Zealand, where hockey remains a small blip on the sporting landscape. Sandra, on the other hand, is from a small rural town in eastern Ontario, where hockey is everything. She played ringette when she was young, and as an adult, she coached her elder daughter, Reagan, in that sport. Camryn spent plenty of time at the rink, watching. "She was dragged to every rink all over the province, and she was a great little cheerleader. But at the beginning, she didn't have a chance to do that on her own."

Through talking to other parents of children with Down syndrome, Sandra heard about a special needs hockey program called the Capital City Condors. The Condors' mission is to make hockey a game for all kids, including those with cognitive and physical disabilities. It was the perfect program for a little girl like Camryn, who was seven years old when she became a Condor. That's how Sandra Wallace became a hockey mom. "One of my girlfriends bought me a mug that says 'Hockey Mom' on it. And I was like, 'Oh my gosh, you know, I am a hockey mom. I am really a hockey mom!'"

The Condors and the game of hockey have been life-changing for Camryn and Sandra and their entire family. "It is a hockey team, but, you know, it's not a typical hockey team. There's no parent up in the stands with a stopwatch timing their kid's ice time. Or yelling at the coach. All the players are out there to play for the pure joy of the game. I think the families are there for the same reasons: to experience that joy through their kids' eyes and that pride you have in watching your kid achieve something that you thought would never really be a possibility."

Camryn is strong and determined. Her coordination is good. In fact, she shares many qualities with high-level athletes. Sandra says, "You know, Ross and I are pretty sure she would have been an elite athlete, because she works so hard and she is very stubborn. She doesn't give up. She wants to win all the time." Hockey seems to bring out the best in her. It is her sport. Her team. Her time to shine. "She has a big personality," her mother says. "She has a ton of attitude. She's sassy as heck, but she's also really loving, and she's fun to be around. I think that's what I always hope when people see her. I hope that they see who she is and not just what she looks like. Or that they don't just see Down syndrome. Yeah, she's pretty cool."

One of Sandra's favourite hockey memories is of a tournament in 2015 that brought together special needs teams from across North America. For many of the players, it was their first time playing against anyone outside their own hockey family. Sandra remembers it as a big deal. "The warm-up was hilarious because they were skating around like they were a real team, and they were so proud. Then we look over in the corner, and Camryn is down on the ice, and she's doing stretches like NHL players."

The parents of Condors players constantly ask themselves if their kids really understand the game. Icings, offsides, faceoffs—do they get it? At that tournament, one of Camryn's teammates put on a dazzling display. He went end to end with the puck and scored a beauty. On his own net. Sandra says the place went wild with excitement. "We were all laughing and crying and cheering because it was like, he gets it. He went down and scored a goal. And it made perfect sense, because all these years, he'd only taken shots at Condors' goalies. We were so proud."

At that moment, Sandra felt an overwhelming sense of happiness. Camryn was in her element. Both mother and daughter had discovered their happy place. "To see your kid out there playing Canada's game, to have that experience and feel the joy it has brought to so many families and to our family, it's just incredible."

TYSEN LEFEBVRE WAS ALSO at that 2015 tournament, not to play but to perform a ceremonial faceoff. He was fourteen years old and getting plenty of media attention for an ambitious fundraising campaign he had launched. After the Make-A-Wish Foundation flew him to California to meet Adam Sandler, Tysen wanted to give back. He boldly told his mom he was going to raise $1 million to help other kids experience the same kind of gift. Linda says, "For me, even if he only ever raised five thousand dollars, that's five thousand we didn't have before. So it was really a no-lose situation for him."

Tysen never had a doubt. The people at Make-A-Wish helped him host galas and hockey tournaments. By the time he went to that special needs tournament to drop the puck, he was two years into his fundraising efforts and had already raised nearly $400,000. Three years later, he would reach his goal.

Going to the tournament was a game-changer for Tysen. He dropped the puck and met many of the kids who were part of the tournament.

He bonded with them. And his mom couldn't drag him away. "He wanted to be at every single game."

Tysen's physical limitations meant hockey would never be a natural fit, but a random conversation with a coach at the tournament revealed that, just maybe, it was possible. The coach pulled out his iPhone and showed Tysen images of a contraption called the Kaye Trainer, a big aluminum frame with wheels and straps. It offers support and protection, and it's perfect for someone like Tysen. Linda says, "That was pretty much it."

Plenty of Tysen's doctors said it wasn't a good idea, but eventually, a doctor in Toronto saw the benefits that playing hockey could have for Tysen. He signed off on Tysen becoming a Condor.

And just like that, Linda Lefebvre was a hockey mom. "We went right from the hospital to the nearest sporting goods store to get all of his hockey equipment. We never looked back."

THAT SPRING, TWO UNLIKELY hockey journeys came together. Camryn Wallace, a few years younger than Tysen, was by then a veteran member of the Condors family. Her mother, Sandra, was in the stands the first time Tysen stepped onto the ice with the help of his Kaye Trainer. "There was not a dry eye in the arena," Sandra says. "Just to see Tysen on the ice was so incredible."

It was almost surreal for Linda and Scott Lefebvre as they watched their son become part of a hockey team. "I never thought I would ever be a hockey mom, but I feel pride." When she saw her son on the ice for the first time, the emotion was overwhelming. "It's not just the hockey, but it's just the fact that he was going to be able to belong somewhere, belong to a team with other kids. A lot of his friends from high school and grade school were playing hockey. He would tell them, 'I have hockey tomorrow.' People just kind of look at him like, 'You play hockey?'"

Her experience as a hockey mom, she realizes, is different from what most moms go through. But in a good way. "Even in tournaments, every goal is celebrated. It doesn't matter what team gets it. It's all just joy. We're just a big hockey family, and it's really nice to be able to have that experience."

It is hard not to get sucked into the Condors experience. It happened to NHL forward Kyle Turris, who became an honorary captain of the Condors when he played in Ottawa. When he was traded to Nashville in 2018, the Condors were devastated. Then Turris invited the whole team to visit him in Nashville. They all went. Sandra Wallace calls it a trip of a lifetime. "That whole experience was huge. All of them dragging their bags around the airport. Those memories are so cool. You can't even express the importance of what that brought to Camryn's life. That feeling of team and camaraderie and the love of the game. Pretty cool, you know."

HOCKEY MOMS. FOR BOTH Sandra Wallace and Linda Lefebvre, it feels good to call themselves that. It feels good, Sandra says, to be living it. "So many Canadian kids dream of playing in the NHL. It's like a religion for Canadians. I think it's truly magical that they are out there. And they are so joyful to be out there and part of a team."

For Sandra, Camryn's hockey experience has been life-changing. "The first time she scored, we had tears coming down." She has cried watching Camryn, she has cheered, she has been moved in ways she never would have imagined. "I've probably grown a lot through Camryn's hockey."

She has watched her daughter grow into a kind and spirited young woman. "That day when they told us that Camryn had Down syndrome, I didn't know what to expect and what it would mean for our family. You wish you could turn back time, because you have all those terrible thoughts and scary feelings when it happens. Now I look back, and she has brought so much joy to our family, and the Condors have been such a big part of that. And I truly believe that exposing our older daughter, Reagan, to programs like the Condors has made her a better person. Would I change Camryn? No. Would I like to be able to change the world sometimes? For sure. Especially how they perceive people like Camryn."

Hockey has also been life-changing for Linda, who feels like every time Tysen plays, she has a front-row seat to hockey at its purest. "I think, ultimately, kids start playing hockey for the love of the game. And we should never lose sight of that. I have no trouble with kids playing and being competitive. But make sure it's always for the kids."

AFTERWORD

BY THERESA BAILEY

It is Sunday, March 8, 2020. The rink has cleared over the last hour, and now I am the last person left in the arena, except for the rink staff and my oldest son, who is taking his sweet time leaving the dressing room. As far as I know, this was his last minor hockey game ever. His team just lost in overtime in game five of the OMHA U18 semifinals. They took it as far as they could. It was an intense and emotional game, the kind where I had to leave the packed stands and watch from the corner with a friend. Momentum had been back and forth, but when their opponent got a breakaway late in the second overtime, you just knew what was coming next.

The jubilation and the defeat. The throwing of sticks and gloves, and the dogpile on top of a helpless goalie. And on our end of the ice, players on their knees, deflated, or leaning against the boards, heads slumped, pausing to regain composure and contemplating what went wrong. For many of them, like my son, it might have been their last game.

As I wait in the arena lobby, the last fifteen years of rinks and hotels and restaurants and car rides and friendships flash before my eyes. How could it all be over so fast? I don't know how to be a parent without it.

Not long ago, I met with a group of youth workers and clinicians who were discussing strategies to connect with vulnerable youth. Having to adapt their methods during COVID-19, they learned that the simple act of taking a youth for a car ride meant that the youth would open up almost effortlessly about all sorts of things. It was their best opportunity to talk, the clinicians said. "Hockey moms have known that all along," I thought. That's what makes those car rides worth every second.

While I wait for my son, I picture the munchkin I took on the ice for the very first time as a two-year-old—his tiny little skates coupled with his total surprise and then frustration that he couldn't just take off like the pros. I look up as he exits the dressing room, now towering over me at six-foot-three. For a seventeen-year-old boy becoming a man, there is nothing worse than an emotional mom, but I've got a lump in my throat and am fighting back tears.

We walk in silence and he avoids my eyes. "I can't believe we lost that one," he says as we step outside.

"I thought you had it" is all I can offer.

He stops walking and looks at me. "I can't believe it's over. Thank you for everything."

Every emotion I've ever had as a parent hits me full in the chest. This journey has always been about hockey, yet none of it is really about hockey at all. I've never understood that more than I do in this minute.

"I know," I say. "Thank you for everything. I have loved every minute of watching you play."

ACKNOWLEDGEMENTS

THIS BOOK WOULD NOT have been possible without the generosity of all of the hockey moms we interviewed for it. Thank you, first and foremost, to all of the moms who shared their stories.

Karen Bailey

Alexandria Briggs-Blake

Lauren Camper

Kristen Crouse

Trina Daigneault

Debbie Doom

Chris Duchene

Kim Gabriel

Brigitte Goure

Lisa Haley

Rhonda Henley

Michelle Hollett

Lisette Kingo

Terri Konecny

Kathy Lee

Linda Lefebvre

Tabatha Leonard

Brenda Little

Ema Matthews

Kelly McDavid

Betsy Mikkelson

Brenda Morrison

Marj Morrison

Theresa Morrison

Carol Nicholson

Jen O'Brien

Jeanna Oke

Bonnie O'Reilly

Chantal Oster-Tkachuk

Jacinda Perrott

Kelly Perrott

Tania Pimm

Nicole Ratt

Manon Rhéaume

Nicole Rhéaume

Donna Rishaug

Shawleen Robinson

Darlene Shaw

Jacqueline Smith

Gloria Sobb

Brenda Steiger

Liza Stekolnikova

Karen Sylvester-Ceci

Sue Taylor

Katie Wakely

Sandra Wallace

Anna Weatherston

Donna Young McCormick

And a special thank you to Bobby Ryan for sharing your mom's story. She would be proud.

FROM TERRY MARCOTTE

I retired from nearly forty years of television news just as COVID hit our world. For the past two decades I had covered sports. I once did a story on Theresa, my co-author, and her website, canadianhockeymoms. ca. She was convinced there was a book waiting to be written about the stories of the mothers she was meeting. I thought so too. When I stepped away from television, I asked if she wanted some help with her book idea. Here we are.

We had just one face-to-face meeting as we carried out Zoom calls with moms from around the world and set out to share their stories. COVID provided challenges, but we got it done. Thank you, Theresa, for putting your trust in me. And for your patience.

My friends in the sports community have provided amazing support. Chris Stevenson, Roy MacGregor, Randy Steinman, Sylvain St. Laurent, Marc Brassard, Brent Wallace, Ian Mendes, A.J. Jakubec, Dan Seguin, James Boyd, Ryan Rishaug, Darren Dreger, and James Duthie are among the many who have shared ideas and contacts that helped pull this book together.

James Duthie and I worked together years ago in Ottawa and have maintained our friendship. When I told him about this project, he reached out to his editor at HarperCollins. Brad Wilson took us on and kept our ship sailing with his wisdom and his patience.

My family has been there for me too. My wife, Lyne, battled breast cancer as the book was coming together. They were difficult times. We got through it together. Our children, Gabrielle and Natalie, were with us too—with their mom and with me as we faced our challenges.

Then there are the mothers who generously shared their stories. I hope we did justice to all you have done to help your sons and daughters grow in the hockey world.

And finally, thank you to my own mom, Marian. She's ninety-six now and still playing the piano with the best of them. Every day, it seems, she would ask, "How is the book coming along?" Every day I would tell her, "It's getting there."

Finally, it's here. Thank you to all who have helped make it happen.

FROM THERESA BAILEY

A lot can get done when you aren't running to the rink five to seven nights a week, and while COVID-19 decimated hockey seasons everywhere, I know for sure that I could not have completed this book had I been running the roads as usual.

There were a lot of people who helped will this book into reality. The first interviews took place way back in 2018, with the help of Nathan Perrott. Thank you for believing strongly enough in the importance of these stories to get me started.

I also want to thank my Wednesday night COVID crew, Tabatha Leonard, Angela Bailey, and Angela Harvey, who helped me work through ideas and always provided the hockey mom perspective to keep me on track. So many more of my hockey mom friends provided insight along the way and reminded me of questions for each of our mothers. Thank you for that, and for the insights about hockey you have shared with me through the years.

Bryant McBride, Gavin Regan, and Paul Carson, thank you for your time and wisdom. Our conversations helped to fill out some important context around the stories.

I've known Terry for a long time, and when he offered in 2020 to help me continue this journey, I jumped at the chance. The speed with which the book came together once we became co-authors was truly unbelievable. Terry, I know I couldn't have gotten this done without you, so thank you.

I'm also grateful to Brad Wilson, our editor at HarperCollins, for your patience and thoughtful feedback through this whole process. Being a hockey dad gave you the experience and understanding to complement your technical knowledge, and I was so appreciative of that understanding. And to the whole team at HarperCollins, thank you for your patience and professionalism and for giving us a chance.

The passion that led me to write a book like this comes directly from my parents, Harold and Karen. They showed me early on the power and beauty of hockey in our small community. I am who I am because of them.

For my children, Kobe, Kellen, and Shea, I know you don't know what I do for work half the time, but you definitely got behind me writing this book. You all know you were my inspiration to write it. I could not be more proud or grateful to have been able to share your hockey journeys through the years. We think that hockey is about a player's development, but the truth is, the parents are growing up right alongside the kids. You've taught me a lot.

Thank you to Ken, and all the hockey dads. We were asked so often to be sure to thank the dads. We have always known the importance of everything you do to keep kids in hockey.

For all the mothers we interviewed, I am forever grateful to you for your time and insights. Interviewing each of you brought such joy and a sense of connection, and that was even more valuable through these isolating times.

For the thousands of hockey moms who have been part of the canadianhockeymoms.ca community over the last decade, thank you. It's not always easy being a woman in the hockey world, but I know the work you do. You are the force behind getting those kids up in the morning, fed, and to the rink. You are the heart of the game.

❧

I intend to donate a portion of my proceeds from the book to the following: The Carnegie Initiative (**www.carnegieinitiative.com**), an initiative created to ensure that hockey is inclusive, supportive, and welcoming to all; and The Angel Project (**www.theangelproject.ca**), which harnesses the power of the hockey community to raise money to support patients in complex care.